RICHARD DEMARCO
A Life in Pictures

RICHARD DEMARCO

A Life in Pictures

An *ArtWork* Special from
Northern Books

An *ArtWork* special publication from Famedram Publishers, who also print and publish the North's indendent arts newspaper, *ArtWork*. Further details: PO Box 3 AB41 9EA
© Drawings and te xt, copyright 1995 Richard Demarco and F amedram Publishers Limited.
No reproduction in any form without the e xpress permission of the publishers.
ISBN 0905 489543

Introduction

THIS is a book in which words and pictures are entwined to tell the story of an artist's life spent in contemplation not only of his own pictures but those of countless others.

As an artist he is represented in over 1500 public and private collections, including the Scottish National Gallery of Modern Art and the Victoria and Albert Museum. In the early 70s he was elected to membership of the Royal Scottish Society of Painters in Watercolours and the Society of Scottish Artists.

The book has a basic chronological structure which conjures up in one's mind a voyage of discovery in four stages: *Setting Forth, At Anchor, Storm Bound* and *Open Seas*.

The text takes the form of essays, memoranda and diaries. Comments have been added with hindsight at the end of 1995, looking back over six decades.

The words encapsulate reminiscences, memories, hopes, fears, dilemmas, ideals: documenting collaborations and friendships with innumerable artists, actors, writers, musicians, gallery and theatre directors, scientists, politicians, historians, philosophers, theologians, school and university teachers and students.

It is a record of countless expeditions and travels in what has come to be known as *The Road to Meikle Seggie,* the road linking the Hebrides to the Cyclades, and bridging the gap between East and West Europe: the old road known to the Romans, Picts and Celts, the builders of Calanais and the Maltese Temples of Hagar Qim.

From 1992 it is also a documentation of the life of a Kingston University professor wishing to forge cultural links between Kingston-upon-Thames, Edinburgh and Derry with the beleaguered cities of Sarajevo and Tuzla.

In the final part of the book, *Open Seas,* the format becomes more experimental to emphasise the fact that sailing in open seas conjures up new horizons with the need always to change course, heeding Joseph Beuys's words that always – 'New Beginnings are in the Offing.'

In this section the words and the drawing become one indivisible form of mark-making.

THIS DRAWING OF A
SLEEPING SOLDIER.
WAS MADE WHEN
I MYSELF WAS
WEARING THE UNIFORM
OF A SERGEANT.
INSTRUCTER IN THE
ROYAL ARMY
EDUCATIONAL CORPS.
TRAVELLING OVER-
NIGHT FROM THE
RAOC CAMA AT
BICESTER VIA
BIRMINGHAM
TO EDINBURGH
ON A 48-
HOUR
LEAVE

SLEEPING SOLDIER ON THE BIRMINGHAM TO EDINBURGH NIGHT TRAIN
Richard DeMarco 1956

MARK MAKING

Mark making: that is all there is to it.
In the making of drawing, painting, any art form
Whatever the medium, the testing is in
Physical energy release – that's it
But with something added – unforgettable
That extra thing that will not be beckoned easily
Or reckoned with or revived.

Energy release, through finger tip and wrist;
At one with eye and heart,
Marking time passing, marking space
Between mind, thinking, hand moving, eye glancing
Never forgetting Lascaux caves or Newgrange spirals
Where first rules were set for da Vinci and for Beuys
Exacting, precise, demanding acrobatic skill,
Articulation of arm and shoulder
Imposing points of balance.
Stone on stone was all that mattered.
Equal to paint on canvas, ink on paper,
Equal to the rapidograph's biting edge.

It all comes down to knowing how to dance;
Wanting and needing to dance
In and out of present time,
Through past and towards future dancing
  – Towards future mark making.

SELF PORTRAIT AS AN ART STUDENT
EDINBURGH 1951

setting
Forth

I often wonder why I, with the Latin temperament of all my forebears, should now be so completely at home in a city whose character is so essentially northern; surely the classicism of the Latin mind would be in conflict with the romanticism of the Scot?

When younger, I deeply resented this conflict and longed for a southern way of life; but this very conflict can be a source of real artistic energy, the: response to the challenge of resolving the problems posed by a classical vision of romantic visual material.

I know now that I am completely at home in Edinburgh in a way I could never be in any Italian city, but part of my pride in her is rooted in the fact that I know it can rank beside those great cities of Italy to which all the world pays homage; I am committed to Edinburgh, to her paintability, in a way which makes any disfigurement of her identity cause me dismay beyond words. "This is my city!" To live in a living, breathing city is to be part of an adventure.

Edinburgh is in many ways still a capital, still the expression of a sophisticated and strongly-defined culture and way of life. In the many layers of history is still embedded much that is best in the Scottish experience as well as the constant fertilisation of European experience. It is a cultural process that is still going on to this day, and thus living in Edinburgh is to be part of a very special adventure – that of the expression of a national culture which has given much to the world and received much from the world and will assuredly continue to do so.

And all this I will not leave.

From New Saltire review, August 1962

VIEW OF EDINBURGH CASTLE FROM 29 FREDERICK ST.   1957

Richard DeMarco

THE FREDERICK STREET FLAT WAS PART OF A GEORGIAN BUILDING.
IT WAS A TOP FLOOR ATTIC FLAT AND FROM ITS WINDOWS A SPLENDID VIEW
COULD BE ENJOYED OF EDINBURGH CASTLE. IT WAS HERE FROM 1957 UNTIL THE
OPENING OF THE TRAVERSE THAT THOSE WHO HELPED JIM HAYNES FEEL 'AT HOME', IN
EDINBURGH AND WHO REPRESENTED AN INTERNATIONAL GROUP OF FRIENDS FOUND
THEMSELVES WANTING THE EDINBURGH FESTIVAL SPIRIT TO EXTEND ALL YEAR ROUND.

IT COULD BE SAID THAT WE MET SATURDAY NIGHT PARTIES GIVEN BY RICHARD AND ANNE DEMARCO ON A REGULAR BASIS FROM 1957 TO 19...

IT WAS AT 29 FREDERICK STREET THAT RICHARD DEMARCO- FIRST INTRODUCED JOSEPH BEUYS AND TADEUSZ KANTOR TO EACH OTHER

AT 29 FREDERICK STREET HELPED PROVIDED THE UNCLUTTERED... FOR THE TRAVERSE THEATRE

IT WAS AT THE 1957 EDINBURGH FESTIVAL THAT JIM HAYNES SHALL MET RICHARD AND DOUGLAS COLTART AND ANNE DEMARCO COLIN COLTART JACK THOMSON COLLECTION.

IT WAS AT 29 FREDERICK STREET THAT COUNT GIUSEPPE PANZA DI BIUMO TO COUNT OF HIS COLLECTION

The Champs Elysées was as broad as I remembered; the posters above the entrances to the de luxe cinemas were as big and eye-catching as ever; a cup of coffee at the exclusive George the Fifth Café still cost a goodly sum when one wanted to sit and watch the world walk by.

All the women in sight were the personification of the desirable creatures who only seem to exist in the eye of the fashion artist and to grace the pages of *Vogue* or *Harper's*. As in crossing the danger-fraught extent of the Concorde, the same principles, or lack of them, apply when a pedestrian attempts to cross the terrifying width which separates the island which forms the Arc de Triomphe from the comparative safety of the top of the Champs Elysées.

When one is in the middle of the road and cars are converging on every side, and all seems to be lost, the best plan is to close one's eyes, offer some suitable orison and continue walking. The pedestrian will find, surprisingly enough, that this apparently drastic and suicidal expedient will nevertheless enable him to make the crossing and that, in effect, it is no more dangerous than to traverse this seemingly impassable roundabout with the eyes open.

It was no wonder that, having reached my destination, I could not force my tired and trembling legs to make the ascent of the narrow stairs that lead to the top of the Arc de Triomphe and the wonderful and magnificent views of the boulevards which radiate from L'Étoile like the broad beams that emanate from a star. Instead, I was satisfied to direct my weary steps to the nearest Métro station with my mind filled with thoughts of a fine dinner cooked in the best tradition of French cuisine and happy in the knowledge that my dreams would be garnished with the lasting images of the marvellous panorama which had unfolded itself before me throughout this perfect day.

From Paris Diary, 1952

"Le Rouquet." café on the Boulevard
18th Sept.   St. Germain

It would indeed be criminal for any tourist to forgo a visit to Montmartre, the very mention of which spells excitement and romance. However, judging from the number of tourists, mostly American and British, who flock to that Mecca, I doubt very much if Montmartre has been unvisited by anyone who has stayed, or even passed through, Paris.

The hill on which this picturesque district of Paris stands is very steep and in some parts almost precipitous. There are many narrow streets and long winding rows of steps to climb before one reaches the summit, on which stands in crowning majesty and shimmering white beauty of the Basilica of the Sacré Coeur.

Warm cream under the strong Paris sun and cold silver in the brightness of flood-lighting, it is significant to me that the Sacré Coeur dominates the hill of Montmartre and the nefarious districts that surround it, for it seems that there, overlooking man's turpitude and worldliness, is the glorious temple of God offering a haven to the world-weary, consolation to the sufferer, and comfort to the sinner if they but care to lift their eyes to the gleaming minarets that rise above the huddle of buildings that constitutes Montmartre.

Sunshine and crowds of people together flooded the Place du Tertre and the precincts of the Sacré Coeur, but even the apparent surfeit of commercialisation has not succeeded in destroying, or in any way submerging, the old-world atmosphere with which Montmartre is imbued.

On every side artists are busy at their easels and in every street there are little shops which advertise for sale their doubtful masterpieces. Whilst watching one young artist at work I noticed that the wall beside him, and on which he was cleaning his brushes, was completely covered with every shade of oil paint, mute testimony of the innumerable artists who had painted the scene before him.

From Paris Diary, 1952

As soon as possible I made my way to the Boulevard Saint Michel, known in student slang as the 'Boul Mich', for I was anxious to revive three-year old memories of when I had last stayed in the Latin Quarter.

The Boul Mich had not changed and I doubt if it ever will. So familiar were the sights and scenes that met my eyes that I found it difficult to reconcile the passing of time. The same fantastically garbed students, zoot-suited negroes and delicately featured orientals lounged at café tables.

As persistent as ever and still quite ignorant of discouragement, were the irrepressible North African hawkers complete with beret or fez and with rugs over their shoulders and capacious baskets filled to overflowing with cheap leather wallets and cheaper trinkets and many other indescribable knick-knacks.

This district is alive with certain people who considerately concern themselves particularly with the monetary embarrassments experienced by so many British tourists and thus I was not surprised to find a coal-black stranger at my elbow whispering in a husky bass voice, "Eh, boy, you like change pounds for francs ?" Unfortunately for this kind gentleman I did not have a pound.

The closing of the many bookshops disperses the crowds who seem to spend hours perusing the contents of the wide variety of books which are on display outside on the pavement book-stalls, but many people are to be seen crowding round the multi-coloured tables before the open doorways of the garishly lit cafés when they commence their cabarets.

Joining one of these crowds I enjoyed an unrecognisable French version of 'On Top of Old Smoky' rendered by five well-seasoned artists whose leader was a woman whose personality and exuberance well compensated her forty-odd years and faded charms.

The performance of a stout contralto who sang Neapolitan love-songs with surprising subtlety of interpretation received much applause and acclamation from those who sat in the tightly packed and smoke-wreathed interior.

From Paris Diary, 1952

Le Marché des Quatre Saisons.
Avenue de General Leclerc.
12th Sept. '52.   Porte d'Orleans.

I spent forty minutes sketching the bizarre frontage of a boucherie, which as usual was open to the street. The shop was packed with meat of all kinds and there were at least ten whole carcases of sheep and pigs suspended from hooks and decorated in a most grotesque manner with little red rosettes and paper frills. Before I had completed my drawing I was invited into the shop by the butcher, a man whose red, moon face was decorated by an absurdly small moustache and whose awe-inspiring stomach was precariously supported by his striped apron.

Once inside I found myself the centre of an admiring group of shop assistants and customers. This was very gratifying but in reply to their excited remarks and questions I could think of nothing else to say but "Je viens d'Écosse – Je ne comprends pas – Il faut que je parte – Au revoir – Merci – Au revoir." At the Marché des Quatre Saisons in the Avenue de General Leclerc my limited knowledge of French again deserted me when, one by one, the jovial women who owned the barrows, all of which were piled high with all kinds of fruits and vegetables and which crowded the pavements, approached me and on finding that their portly figures were included in my drawing commenced to jabber away in the most colloquial and unintelligible French. An occasional *mais oui* and *certainement* from me when they paused for breath prevented the conversation from being completely one-sided and perhaps gave them the impression, together with my Latin appearance, that I was a rather untalkative French art student.

From my wanderings in this quarter and the others like it on the outskirts of the city, I have learned that the Frenchman still knows the art of conversation and still possesses a palate that appreciates a good wine.

From Paris Diary, 1952

On the day when the pale autumn sun first decided to grin weakly through the clouds I wandered by chance into the exquisite Luxemburg Gardens, which lie at the top of the Boul Mich.

How I regretted that on my previous holidays in Paris I had omitted to visit these Gardens and thus denied myself the pleasures they afford. Having purchased, for the modest fee of ten francs, one of the comfortable little chairs which were strewn all over the pathways, I was content to sit and enjoy the sensuous contentment of the sun, which was becoming warmer as the afternoon progressed.

Soon the sight of the many children who were playing around a large boating pond, which once had formed the main feature of the Gardens of the Royal Palace of Luxemburg, filled me with an unfamiliar paternal delight and interest.

Near the pond *un marchand de ballons* carefully transferred gaily-dancing hydrogen-filled balloons from his barrow into the eager hands of these happy children who were fortunate enough to be able to afford them. If my pocket had allowed such generosity I think that I would have bought every child one of those bright red, pink, blue, green, and yellow balloons.

On the other side of the pond a pleasant-faced man provided friendly rivalry by hiring out small yachts to the very small boys. How well and how confidently they captained their various craft!

Here, thought I, were perhaps some of the great seamen of the coming century. And those with the balloons, so great was their interest and fascination in the whims and fancies of the air, perhaps they would one day know the joys of looping round Mars or exploring the dusty corners of the Milky Way.

From Paris Diary, 1952

The village of Arcueil.
20th Sept. 52.

I had a particular interest in the Italian avant-garde because of my personal experience of what was to become an infamous happening on the 1964 Official Festival programme.

The happening was stage-managed by a combination of the talents of John Calder, the publisher and art patron and Jim Haynes, the American founder of Edinburgh's Traverse Theatre. They had, through their shared interest in world literature, organised a Writers' Conference for the Edinburgh Festival with luminaries such as Kenneth Tynan and Bernard Levin as collaborators.

The conference attracted writers of the calibre of Lawrence Durrell, Henry Miller, Norman Mailer, L.P. Hartley, J.B. Priestly, Lillian Hellman, Muriel Spark, Jack Gelber and William Burroughs.

Amidst these literary world luminaries there were to be found the American artist Allen Kaprow, whose very name personified the happening in the United States, and the Scottish artist, Mark Boyle, who was among the very first instigators of happenings in Britain, and the American theatre director Charles Marowitz.

The Writers' Conference happening caused the spirit of the avant-garde to explode in the heart of the official Edinburgh Festival It prepared the way for the Traverse Theatre and therefore the Demarco Gallery to come into being. It was the one Edinburgh Festival event that I could remember with which I knew Piero Manzoni could have been identified.

Foreword to Roma Punta Uno, 1988

JIM HAYNES AND
HIS FRIEND
BEN LASSERS
+ AN AMERICAN
MEDICAL STUDENT
WITNESSING
THE EVENT
BESIDE THE
PAPERBACK'S
MASCOT —
THE RHINOCERUS.

ON A DAY
WHEN
OVERNIGHT
SNOW BEGAN
TO THAW.

THE BURNING OF LADY CHATTERLY'S LOVER OUTSIDE THE
PAPERBACK BOOKSHOP BY AN EDINBURGH LADY, A FORMER AFRICAN
MISSIONARY WHO HAD COME WELL-PREPARED WITH A JAR OF
METHYLATED SPIRITS.
RICHARD DEMARCO

I wanted a mutual dialogue to be cultivated between Scotland and Italy for the simple reason that I was born in Edinburgh as an Italo-Scot; that is, into the community of Italians who had decided to live and work in Scotland.

The Italians had first come in significant numbers to Scotland in the last ten to fifteen years of the 19th century. By the first decade of the 20th century they numbered almost 25,000, centred chiefly in Glasgow and Edinburgh. For inexplicable reasons these Italian immigrants began their journeys to Scotland from two locations in Italy.

The Demarcos seemed to have begun their wanderings north-westwards from Italy from the Province of Frosinone and in particular from the small mountain village of Piciniso 50 miles south of Rome.

The Fuscos, my mother's family, had their origins in the Tuscan region, centred on the small hill-town of Barga, not so far from Lucca.

Even as a child being brought up in Edinburgh, I had a sense of Scotland being linked to the world of my Italian forbears for the simple reason that even at primary school I learned that the Romans had landed at the mouth of a small river called the Almond, six miles from Edinburgh's city centre, and there they had established what was to be the main supply-base for the building of the final North-Western frontier of the Roman Empire the wall of the Emperor Antonine. It was built 120 miles North of Hadrian's Wall which linked the estuaries of the Solway and the Tyne, and in so doing defined the modern border between Scotland and England.

The Antonine Wall linked the estuaries of the two great Scottish rivers, the Forth and the Clyde. I had always been inspired by the thought of the centre of the European Mediterranean world touching the periphery of Europe, in the form of the Celtic and Pictish culture of Scotland.

It seemed to make sense of my Italian origins. I delighted in the thought of the Emperor Septimus Severus having once momentarily ruling the Roman Empire from Cramond, accompanied by his 11-year-old son Caracalla.

To this day, on the beach at the mouth of the Almond, you can still see the Eagle Rock. This represents the eagle, which, of course, is the the emblem of the Ninth Legion – the legendary Lost Legion, which disappeared without trace when it dared to move northwards toward the Grampian mountains.

Even to this day this mountain range marks the boundary of the Highland or Celtic speaking world of Scotland, separating it from the English speaking Scottish Lowland world which surrounds Edinburgh, set in the terrain appropriately known as the Lothians.

Foreword to Roma Punta Uno, 1988

MAIN STREET
PICINISCO

Richard Demarco

In the first year of the Demarco Gallery's life I made a point of visiting Rome to meet Maria Alfani, who ran a small private gallery. Through her kindness I was able to see for myself the complexity of the fast developing contemporary art world in Rome. I visited for the first time the Galleria Nazionale d'Arte Moderna.

The fates ordained that my dialogue with Italy continued with the friendships I developed in the seventies with Alessandra Marchi, Director of the Centro Di, in Florence, Gabriella Cardazzo, Director of the Galleria Cavallino in Venice, and Giuseppe Panza, Italy's most progressive art patron in Varese, and with Dr. Rudi Fuchs as Director of the Palazzo Reale di Rivoli, near Turin. Thus my attention was drawn towards the north of Italy.

This year after presenting an exhibition by the Torino-based artist Mario Merz in March the focus moves again southwards with the gallery's presentation for the Edinburgh Festival of the La Zattera Di Babele production of *Towards MacBeth – A Prologue*. This involved the gallery in working with the founders and creators of La Zattera di Babele – Carlo Quartucci and Carla Tatò.

I had first enjoyed their work as defenders of avantgardism in the performing arts after I first saw them at the Venice Biennale in 1984. They are based in Rome and Sicily, and can therefore lay sound claims to being representative of that culture which is of the Mezzo Giorno.

Now with the exhibition Roma Punto Uno the dialogue continues to move South to Rome, where the dialogue I had first sought with Italy began.

I am grateful indeed to Edinburgh's Italian Cultural Institute for giving me the opportunity to have such a dialogue, and indebted to Dr. Alberto di Mauro its most energetic and innovative director.

Foreword to Roma Punta Uno, 1988

BARGA STEPS   Richard Demarco 90

Born an Italo-Scot, my birthright was European. This was both fortunate and unfortunate. Fortunate because I first knew the taste of Europe in my mother's pasta, and minestrone and unfortunate because, when Italy declared war on the Allies, I was beaten up by those children in my primary school playground who recognised me as the personification of a European enemy by the very colour and texture of my skin and hair.

It has always been so: this mixture of advantage and disadvantage, but as the years roll by to the eighties and nineties, being an Italo-Scot began to give me a headstart in the race that all Scots must now run towards the beckoning image of a New Europe, in which memories of The Berlin Wall receed to the point of incredulity.

So why, as a fully Europeanised Scot on the eve of the 1994 Edinburgh Festival do I feel ill-at-ease, with a distinct sense of frustration and even foreboding?

Is it because in the heady years of the sixties which gave birth to The Traverse Theatre and The Demarco Gallery, doorways were opening and opportunities presented despite the fact that half of Europe was in a state of enslavement?

The Edinburgh Festival-goer who walked through the doors of the newly opened Traverse Theatre could smell a whiff of legitimate European cultural internationalism hard to find in the programmes of most Festival Fringe venues.

Today the Fringe brochure listing hundreds of productions records an infestation of stand-up comics and a dearth of Shakespeare and more seriously a lack of theatre in those languages which express the spirit of the New Europe, those which had to deal unwillingly with communism.

In 1963, the forces of the market-place did not apply to Fringe venues, and neither did the voice of despair expressed in the despairing routines of stand-up comics using Edinburgh as a launching pad for their television careers in the English speaking world.

The Festival, more than any other factor in Scottish cultural life, gave me proof, that as an Edinburgh citizen, born and bred, I could live to the full, the life of a European cosmopolite. My experience of the Festival, even if it was restricted to three weeks a year, from 1947 onwards, adds up to one hundred and forty-one weeks, or two and a quarter years of relishing Edinburgh as the undisputed European capital of culture.

Despite this gift bestowed upon me and generations of Edinburgh citizens by an Austrian Jew, Rudolph Bing, and an Ulsterman, Tyrone Guthrie, the Scots seem nowadays uncomfortable with the challenge of the final decade of the twentieth century. This must include the dream of a Europe freed at long last from the two opposing political ideologies which created the concept of a communism in the East and materialistic monetarism in the West.

ARSENALE CANAL, VENEZIA   RICHARD DEMARCO 90

Ex cathedra is the way in which the Supreme Pontiff, the Bishop of Rome speaks from the Cathedra Petri to that part of the world defined by the Christo-Judaic culture into which I was born and from which developed the concept of the modern city. This culture has given the world the atom bomb to contend with, but to offset the negative implications of that, it has also given what is generally known as the spirit of avant-gardism in 20th century art through music, dance and the visual arts.

Born as I was in the last years of that age of religious faith which still existed in Europe more or less halfway between the two World Wars, I was always in awe of Rome, that city from which a human being could be given the divine power of speaking *ex cathedra*.

My father's family name suggested that my forebears were followers of someone called 'Marcus'. I often wondered if they followed him to Scotland and if he was associated with that Roman Legion that managed to get itself thoroughly lost in the Scottish Highlands.

They had originated in fact from the Province of Frosinone, just 60 miles south of Rome. My father was rightly proud of his Roman origins. They represented an imperial power strong enough to mark its extreme North Western boundary by a line connecting the estuaries of the Rivers Forth and Clyde called the Antonine Wall. This was the landscape to which my father's parents and countless other Italian families had been inexplicably drawn in the last years of the 19th century.

I had the sense of living on a periphery all the days of my youth. I knew I was born in Edinburgh, a city which marked the site of a kingdom opposed to encroachment from an imperial power, the kingdom ruled by a king called Edwin linking what is now called Northumbria with the Lowlands of Scotland and which was doubtless associated through a potent mixture of history and mythology to Arthur, that arch enemy of Rome, the once and future king of all the Celtic peoples of Europe.

To this day his name endures in the form of a magic mountain which dominates the centre of Edwin's capital or 'burgh', that mountain called 'Arthur's Seat', the 'cathedra' of Arthur. It is in fact a grass covered hill almost 1000 feet high, but because of its peculiar and perfectly proportioned shape it is easy to imagine it as the site of that city of perfection associated with the name 'Camelot'. It is formed by nature with extraordinary accuracy and refinement to look like a recumbent lion. It has always been for me one of the wonders of the world, the equal, in its mystery and beauty to the Sphinx of Egypt

All that is left nowadays of this 'Seat of Arthur' are rows of earthen terraces cut into the South Eastern slopes. Long after Arthur's reign the medieval city of Edinburgh grew around an outcrop of volcanic rock which forms the stuff and substance of this magic mountain. The outcrop now known as Castle Hill was obviously the perfect place for Edwin's successors to build their citadel around which a city could form itself.

THE TOWERS OF SAN GIMIGNANO
AS VIEWED FROM "LA ROCCA"

Richard Demarco
1991

The war years made it difficult for me to imagine myself experiencing the continental culture which my parents embodied. My whole childhood was blighted by the role that Italy was obliged to enact in world affairs until peace finally came. In 1949, the last year of my schooldays, I was able to go as far as Paris, the capital city even then for the world's artists containing as I imagined a fountain-head of truth from which aspiring art students could drink their fill and thus claim a place in the post-war international art world.

At the end of my first year at Edinburgh College of Art, wishing to celebrate my 20th birthday in relation to the worldwide celebrations of the Holy Year of 1950, I embarked, in the company of my father and 30 other pilgrims from Britain on my first journey to Italy and to Rome. We travelled by train, Cross-Channel Ferry and bus, through Paris across the Alps to Rome, and when I first experienced the sight of a vast crowd assembled within St. Peter's Square to receive the blessing of Pope Plus XII, I knew for the first time the true meaning of the word city as centre, not only of a national culture but of a world religion.

I soon realised that the crowd-filled piazza under the roof of a brilliant blue Roman sky was not quite the centre of the world. It was designed by Gianlorenzo Bernini, the archetypal Rennaissance artist as the architect, sculptor, painter, capable of accepting the responsibility of designing the 'Cathedra Petri' the throne of Peter as the focal point upon which the location of the High Altar is fixed.

It was only when I entered St. Peter's and knelt before that High Altar that I understood the full implications of the word altar as the 'sanctum sanctorum' of any city and Rome in particular as 'The Eternal City'. Tens of thousands of people from every country imaginable had gathered to pray in one language before the steps of Bernini's High Altar under Michaelangelo's vast dome, the ultimate definition of sculptural space, in the presence of the Pope himself.

It was my first experience of the 'total art work' involving religious ritual and sculpture on a gigantic-scale . It was •••• created for the best possible reason. Of course by 1950 •••• I must have benefited from three years' experience of Edinburgh transformed by art for three weeks annually into a world capital of culture, through the Edinburgh Festival, established against all the odds in 1947. I knew, therefore that the experience of art was inextricably linked to the experience of a city which was in itself an art work.

Vicolo degli Arci. Vieste (GARGANO)

Archiseo DiMARCO – July
1980

Little did I realise, born and bred as a citizen of Edinburgh, that I was being influenced daily by what could be considered arguably the most beautiful and magnificent city site in all of Northern Europe. I had been taught to consider it as the 'Modern Athens', a title it had earned for itself in the period of the 18th century Enlightenment in Scotland, but knowing as I did, that it was built on seven hills, I preferred to think of it as the Northern European equivalent of Rome, for it was to me, even as a child, a city undeniably and proudly able to define the culture of Europe's North Western periphery, the necessary complement to Rome as the ultimate metropolitan centre of Europe's Mediterranean culture.

My Roman Catholic education taught me to see the pagan power of Rome transformed to facilitate the spread of Christianity throughout the length and breadth of Europe and in spite of the extreme form of Protestantism represented by John Knox, the leader of the Reformation in Scotland, that the bedrock of Scotland's cultural heritage was irreversibly Catholic.

Such an education was inextricably linked with the profound mysteries of orthodox religious ritual and the fact that all time in Europe was measured in relation to the death of Christ upon the Cross of Calvary.

As an altar server and chorister I had personal experience of a world of theatre on a grand scale when it came to the celebration of the great Christian feasts of Christmas and Easter. Every season of the year and every human emotion was taken into account in the sound of eighth Century Gregorian chant and in the words of the De Profundis and in the Litanies of the Saints. The spoken word took upon itself an undeniably poetic dimension because it was beyond the limitations of a vernacular connotation.

Latin as a language was meaningful to me as a form of music. There were the sensual pleasures in the smell of incense and burning candles and in the colours of the priest's vestments and altar adornments.

White and gold, green and purple and black were colours which helped me know with delicate precision each season of the year and the significance of the passing hours of each day.

It was precisely because Edinburgh was such a great distance from Rome that I had felt a deep longing to travel from the European periphery to its centre in the spirit of a pilgrim. I cannot think of a time when I did not want to be an artist of some sort and I felt in my child's heart that my parents spoke the truth when they said that all great art and artists came from Italy and that even Paris and the French culture which they admired was built upon the principles of the Italian Rennaissance.

VIA APPIA - PERUGIA   Richard Demarco 80

Through the combined experience of The Holy Year 1950 and the Edinburgh Festival the word city became identified in my mind with the words art and prayer. I knew that when these three words could be linked significantly I could imagine that God was in His Heaven and that the concept of the Communion of Saints was well defended by those inhabitants of the world who defined themselves as city dwellers.

However, since that Holy Year of 1950, the concept of the city as I had imagined it in my youth is almost impossible to defend after the full impact of four decades of ever increasing materialism spreading through Europe, emanating from the basically Protestant culture of the New World defined by the United States of America.

Sadly, it is the image of New York, not Rome which the politician, the banker and the industrialist have when they conceive of the city's shape in the last part of the 20th century.

Nowhere is this more clearly seen than in London where the towers and skyscrapers of New York's Wall Street have been built anew to deny the very existence of London's equivalent of St. Peter's, the great masterwork of Christopher Wren, St. Paul's Cathedral.

The so-called 'great' American cities are all built upon a fundamental heresy that the city dweller's main function is to worship at the high altar of Mammon to the point where the life of the spirit personified by the cathedral is well nigh obliterated.

When I think of the much vaunted new American cities and their so-called centres in Houston and Dallas, and their British counterparts in Birmingham and Manchester, I cannot think that the word city should be identified with the word 'civilised' or with the age old concept which held sway all over Europe, even into the immediate post-war period, that a city's credentials lay in the dominating presence of its cathedral.

More and more we are faced with the inescapable reality that the arts can be supported only through their capacity to be identified with monetarist value systems. This is so despite the fact that the evidence of European history makes it clear that art can only flourish when the artist is in dialogue with the banker and the merchant through an intermediary in the form of the bishop; praying at his cathedral's high altar.

The Medici alone could not have produced the glories of the Rennaissance in direct dialogue with the artists they admired because governing the Medici thoughts and attitudes and their favourite artists, despite all their wordly power and pride and sinfulness, was the basic universal belief that Mankind's destiny and all human activities were governed by spiritual dimensions.

Evidence for this can be found even to this day in the city centres of Florence, Venice and Sienna where the market place and the seat of the civic government were built within the domain of the cathedral.

COLO DEGLi ARCI. OSTUNI. (GARGANO)   Richard DeMarco 81

If the Scots seem ill-prepared to deal with this time of dramatic and even frightening change, it is perhaps necessary to look back to that period in history when the Reformation caused Scotland to reject the legacy of the Holy Roman Empire. After the Union of the Parliaments and the failure of the Jacobite cause, the Scots seemed content to play the role of empire builders under the dominance of the English dream of a white Anglo-Saxon Protestant culture as far afield as the sub-continent of India and Australasia. In the years between the two World Wars the Scots in cultural matters had little to do with Europe except for the oustanding achievements of Charles Rennie Mackintosh and his circle of artistic friends and their preparedness to be in fruitful dialogue with the Viennese Secessionists.

Scotland's future is undoubtedly no longer related to dreams of empire. Any dreams must be focussed on the Europe which Scotland helped to create. Imagine Europe without the cultural impact of Celtic missionaries and scholars on their heroic journeys southwards from the Atlantic shorelines towards Galicia or the Mediterranean through Provençal hills and even into the European heartland of the Low Countries and the valleys of the Rhine and Ruhr, and Danube leading to the Swiss Valleys and beyond to the plains between the Alps and Venice onwards, via Slovenia into Hungary.

Imagine Scotland without the civilising nature of all the monasteries built to the rule of St Benedict. They created a cultural and religious network from Montecassino to Melrose and Pluscarden!

Imagine a Europe without those students and their teachers who created an equally important network linking the medieval Scottish Universities of St Andrews, Edinburgh and Glasgow with the Sorbonne, Bologna, Padua, Torun, Cracow, Prague and perhaps most importantly with Oxford and Cambridge. This was the network that allowed Duns Scotus to live and work in rural Berwickshire and end his life a much honoured teacher in Paris, known to his fellow scholars as the 'Scotsman', or to be more precise as the 'Irish man from Duns.'

This was the European academic tradition which made possible the polyphonic music poetry comparable to Chaucer associated with three great Scots; Robert Carver, William Dunbar and William Henderson. They communicated not only in broad Scots but also in the international lingua franca of both Church and University, that language which obliged every scholar and artist to consider the origins of European culture embedded in the worlds of Ancient Athens and Rome.

Sadly there is no twentieth century equivalent of Latin, only computer-speak and the Americanised English spoken by the new newsreaders of CNN and MTV. Have the Scots forgotten that their heroic King Robert the Bruce was of Norman lineage, and that there is probably more than a grain of truth in the legend that the Great Pibroch music which the Macrimmons developed on Skye originated in the music schools of Cremona?

Have they forgotten that Edinburgh's New Town was built on the architectural principal of Palladio, as interpreted by the brothers Robert and William Adam. **42/43**

VILLA GNOCCHI-MAVARELLI
NEAR PERUGIA

Despite the terrible legacy of Mussolini's Italy and its damaging effects on the life of my parents and close family relations, I have always considered myself fortunate to be born an Italo-Scot. I was provided with a challenge that has shaped the very nature of my life's work and has caused me instinctively to play the role of an internationalist in Scotland's cultural life.

That is why I immediately rejoiced in the very first Edinburgh International Festival. The key word for me, even as a 17-year-old schoolboy in 1947, was 'international'. The Traverse Theatre was born out of the internationalism of the Festival.

I should know because I was fortunate enough to play a role among those who founded the Traverse. Chief among them was that legendary exile from New Orleans, Jim Haynes, whose whole life is still dedicated to creating a personal international communication system. The Demarco Gallery was born out of the Traverse.

From My Scotland, 1988

RAINSTORM APPROACHING SAN GIMIGNANO.
91

Scotland is to Italy as North is to South, periphery to centre, Celtic to Roman, Atlantic to Mediterranean, Protestant to Catholic. Physically, geographically, psychologically, theologically and culturally, therefore, Scotland and Italy represent two contrasting aspects of Europe. Together, however, they represent the widest possible conception of what it means to be European – with all the complexities inherent in the Judaeo-Christian dynamic, from which still flows the vital energy of the Italian Renaissance and the Scottish Enlightenment.

Two of the most important manifestations of what we now call modernity and progress.

This energy has given the world the Rennie Mackintosh chair and the Olivetti typewriter, the poetry of MacDiarmid and Dante, the theology of Duns Scotus and Thomas Aquinas, the explorations of David Livingstone and Marco Polo. the electrical communications sytems of Graham Bell and Marconi, the novels of Scott and Visconti, the architecture of Adam and Palladio, the medieval universities of St Andrews and Bologna, the pipes of Skye and the violins of Cremona.

The list could be endless: it does not even include the lives of some of the greatest thinkers – Leonardo Da Vinci, Machiavelli, Adam Smith or David Hume, and without their contributions to the history of ideas our modern world is unthinkable.

Such a list gives me no choice but to take seriously my origins as an Italo-Scot. It requires a concept of Europe that is beyond the imagination of far too many Europeans, who believe that the extremes of north and south imply two opposing and irreconcilable ways of life.

From My Scotland, 1988

PIAZZA VECCHIA
RODI·GARGANICO.

There is only one city comparable to Rome I can think of in Britain and that is Edinburgh, because it still possesses the vestiges of a cultural and political capital, and because its architectural shape and history is dominated by a cathedral precinct which is bordered at its highest point by a castle and at its lowest point by an abbey and palace. The cathedral is dedicated, not to a Scottish saint, but to Saint Giles, better known in France as one of that band of Irish missionaries who spread Celtic culture from the Atlantic shore of Europe deep into the Mediterranean.

St. Giles Cathedral is positioned literally at a point known as The Heart of Midlothian defining the centre, not only of Edinburgh as a city, but the whole surrounding area. Its cathedral tower is in the shape of the crown of Charlemagne, an architectural form peculiar to Scotland and evidence of Scotland's close links with the medieval Roman Catholic world all over the European continent.

The St. Giles high altar is located halfway between two other altars marking places of religious pilgrimage. One is in the Abbey of Holyrood and the other is in the chapel of Queen Margaret, the one and only Scottish monarch who attained sainthood. It is the oldest building within the Edinburgh castle walls and rightly built upon the highest point of the Castle Hill. The three altars are linked by what is called the Royal Mile, defining the medieval High Street.

The tiny Romanesque stained glass window behind the altar of Saint Margaret will direct your gaze towards the lowest point of the Royal Mile where the street ends at the altar of King David II, after winding its way down a dramatically curving spine of volcanic rock to what is now called Holyrood Park.

The altar exists within the impressive ruins of Holyrood Abbey adjoining the Palace of Holyrood House for the simple reason that divine intervention caused the life of King David, the grandson of Queen Margaret to be saved when alone and imperilled in the depths of what was then a royal forest, he found himself face to face with a legendary white stag. The stag's life was spared and so too was the King's when, with the stag at bay he was unexpectedly surrounded by a pack of wolves.

At the moment of truth there appeared miraculously between the antlers of the stag a blinding cruciform light which struck terror into the wolves. King David had no choice but to acknowledge the possibility of a miraculous event in the form of an altar built as an act of thanksgiving.

The miracle took place half a mile from where the 12th century city walls had ended at the Netherbow Gate. This gateway is nowadays marked by brass plates embedded in the Royal Mile's cobbles. Appropriately this point is known even to this day as 'World's End' for at that point the city and the life of civilised man ended and the untamed ungovernable, unknown spaces of the wilderness began in the form of the Royal Forest.

ANCHOR CLOSE ROYAL MILE   RICHARD DEMARCO 89

Of course the city had to be extended through succeeding centuries to take into account that point in the forest where the life of the king had been spared and so it is that the medieval city of Edinburgh and its Royal Mile owe their eventual shape, not to the machinations of townplanners , but to an act of divine intervention. This story should be told to anyone wishing to play the role of an Edinburgh Festival-goer, particularly those concerned with what is called the Edinburgh Festival Fringe, because the Fringe was born within the structure of that Royal Mile, in all manner of temporary converted premises in the form of church and school and. masonic temple halls located in the alleyways known as closes and wynds.

One of these halls was converted into Edinburgh's Traverse Theatre. The five year story of how this came to be defines the beginnings of my work as an art gallery and theatre director. The language of art under the aegis of the Edinburgh Festival transformed Edinburgh's Old Town giving the street and buildings new life and meaning.

Edinburgh was chosen as the world capital for art because of the beauty and sacred nature of its historic Old Town fabric.

There is a lesson for all modern architects to be learned in this inescapable truth and it should provide inspiration to those who would wish to build the cities of the third millenium, to accommodate the dimension which art provides in the form of international festivals.

Schools of architecture would have to consider teaching their students how to cope with the phenomenon of what nowadays is called 'performance art' as a manifestation of that need for ritual deep set in the human heart.

In the hands of master artists such as Joseph Beuys, Tadeusz Kantor, Alastair Maclennan and Paul Neagu this form of visual arts expression can work most effectively in helping to focus attention upon the ills which nowadays beset most cities as well as upon the points of high, life-enhancing energy to be found in unexpected aspects and areas of the city's fabric. Most 'performance art' relies heavily upon the physical presence of the artist in confrontation with the audience. The performance artist thus focuses attention upon the sacred nature of the human presence as a measure of all man made things embodied in furniture and architecture as well as all manner of ornaments and implements, utensils, machinery, vehicles, clothing, sound, movement and symbolism.

THINKING ABOUT THE ORIGINS OF THE TRAVERSE THEATRE AND ART GALLERY
RECALLS TO MY MIND A LETTER WHICH THE ARTIST PATRICK REYNTIENS WROTE
TO ME ON 2 JULY. 1975. IT WAS PART OF HIS CONTRIBUTION TO THE DEMARCO
GALLERY'S "EDINBURGH ARTS", EDINBURGH FESTIVAL EXHIBITION CATALOGUE. AN
EXHIBITION WHICH WAS THE FIRST EVER TO TAKE PLACE IN THE BUILDING WHICH
NOW HOUSES THE EDINBURGH CITY ART CENTRE. SUCH A BUILDING, I REMEMBER
THINKING IN 1975, IF IT HAD BEEN AVAILABLE IN 1963 WOULD HAVE SURELY
ATTRACTED THOSE WHO ATTENDED ON THE BIRTH OF THE TRAVERSE WITHIN THE
CONFINES OF THE BASEMENT AND FIRST FLOOR ROOMS OF A JAMES COURT TENEMENT.
HOWEVER, I HAD FORGOTTEN MOMENTARILY HOW THE ORIGINAL TRAVERSE WAS
AN IMPORTANT FACTOR IN ITS SUCCESSFUL BEGINNINGS, BECAUSE IT WAS
AN EXTENSION OF THE DOMESTIC SPACES IN WHICH THOSE WHO CREATED THE
TRAVERSE HAD GATHERED IN FRIENDSHIP FOR YEARS WHILST WAITING
FOR THE OPPORTUNE TIME TO MAKE THEIR IDEAS AND PLANS A REALITY.

IN APRIL 1995
PAINTINGS BY
DOUGLAS CRAFT
AN AMERICAN ARTIST
WHO EXHIBITED
WITH HIS WIFE
ELIZABETH HANNS

THE TRAVERSE GALLERY
ALSO PRESENTED EXHIBITIONS
OF JASPER JOHNS!
OF JASPER JOHNS.

THE TRAVERSE GALLERY WAS
HOUSED IN A TINY ROOM
ABOVE THE TINY THEATRE.
IT WAS DESIGNED BY A
FRIEND — THE ARCHITECT
GEARY WILLOW

THE LETTER BEGAN THUS: "ART SEEMS TO ORIGINATE IN THE
MEETINGS OF FRIENDS. I'VE NEVER HEARD OF OFFICIAL ENCOUNTERS
EVEN ON AN INTERNATIONAL LEVEL WHICH TRULY TRIGGERED
OFF MOVEMENTS AND IDEAS. ONLY FRIENDS AND THINGS
ADMIRED — WHICH IS A KIND OF FRIENDSHIP
THE TRAVERSE DID NOT ORIGINATE IN ANY INTELLECTUAL CONCEPT OF
EXPERIMENTAL THEATRE OR GALLERY, BUT INDEED THROUGH THE MEETINGS OF
FRIENDS.
WITHIN TWO YEARS OF ITS FOUNDING SCOTTISH EXPATRIATE ARTISTS SUCH AS
MARK BOYLE, WILLIAM CROZIER AND WILLIAM JOHNSTONE AS WELL AS
YOUNG SCOTTISH ARTISTS SUCH AS BARBARA BALMER, GEORGE MACKIE, ROBERT
CALLENDER EDWARD GAGE, TOM MACDONALD, MANY MORE GORDON, ALAN DAICHES
FRANCES WALKER, TONY VALENTINE, IAN MACKENZIE-SMITH, ELIZABETH BLACKADDER
JOHN HOUSTON, SANDY FRASER & DAVID MICHIE. ALISTAIR MICHIE THERE WORK WAS SHOWN
AS COMPLEMENTARY ARTISTS, PARTICULARLY IAGO PERICOT FROM SPAIN, TAM MACPHAIL & RICK
ULMAN FROM USA. MARTIN BRADLEY FROM FRANCE, SURJIT SINGH FROM INDIA
ASIRU & TWINS SEVEN-SEVEN FROM NIGERIA.

At
Anchor

The opening exhibition of 57 artists revealed the gallery's intention to place leading Scottish artists in an international context.

There were Phillipson, Blackadder and Houston paintings hanging beside Herons, Waagamakers, Pasmores, Wynters and Tilsons. Jorge Castillo, the celebrated Catalan artist, was then given a one-man exhibition.

The Christmas exhibition reinforced the need for close contact with the London art scene. The Marlborough, Hamilton, Roland, Browse and Delbanco, Redfern, Axiom, Kasmin, Piccadilly and Waddington Galleries were all represented with the widest possible range of work.

David Baxandall, the Director of the National Galleries of Scotland, taking part in the BBC *Arts Review* programme commented: "The Demarco Gallery occupies three floors of a house in Melville Crescent, ingeniously converted to the purposes of a dealer's gallery in the London west-end style.

"The basement has a café which I have not investigated, but the ground floor and first floor are exhibition rooms. In order to give more wall space, the windows have been covered, and you see everything by well arranged artificial light. The walls are all white; the ceilings of the first floor rooms are black. The floors are covered with carpets or rush matting, which is kind to the feet.

"The result is a gallery in which contemporary paintings and sculpture can be seen with ease, presented in the kind of way and kind of environment in which they look their best.

"The opening exhibition showed a selection of the kind of work you might find in a London gallery that deals with the more up-to-date and fashionable manifestations of modern painting and sculpture. They are mostly English works, a few Scottish, and the odd American, Frenchman or Swede. There is also a fairly large portfolio of modern lithographs with splendid prints by Ceri Richards and Piper and Pasmore, which is a most welcome addition to the cultural market here.

"For the first time in Scotland we have a dealer's gallery that sets out to show a changing selection of the sort of work that painters, sculptors and collectors find most interesting at the present day in the big world outside Scotland. It seems to me that this is a most healthy and beneficial thing. Modern Scottish painting has many virtues but a good deal of it suffers from the effects of in-breeding. We all know the sort of painting that has been called 'Edinburgh school', in which pleasant colour is combined with skill in handling paint broadly but tastefully, decoratively rather than expressively.

"Any painter who follows this style in Scotland is fairly sure of support from the picture-buying public; it is the accepted and established thing. As a result many painters have produced variations on the styles of the leading local painters here in Scotland and a very cosy time is had by all. It is just a little parochial and it doesn't have all that much to do with the main current of contemporary painting.

"For this reason any gallery that can keep us in touch with what is happening in the big world is a tremendously significant addition to our cultural life. We don't have to accept it all as of equal importance, but at least we have a chance of becoming more aware of it... It could be a real stimulus to the painters and a source of education to the picture-buying public."

Richard Demarco Gallery 1966-76: 1966

NUMBER 8 MELVILLE CRESCENT, HOUSED THE DEMARCO GALLERY FROM 1966 UNTIL 1973 — SEVEN EVENTFUL YEARS IN A WELL-NIGH PERFECT, ELEGANT NEW TOWN HOUSE

IN 1970 THIS GALLERY HOUSED AN EXHIBITION ENTITLED 'NEW DIRECTIONS'

"NEW DIRECTIONS" WAS A CONTEMPORARY EXPRESSION OF THE "AVANT-GARDE" IN SCOTLAND AND
— A RESPONSE TO THE ELECTRIFYING AVANT-GARDE OF THE DÜSSELDORF ARTISTS EXPRESSED "CONTACTS-GET-ARTS"

ROMANIAN ARTIST HORIA BERNEA PAUL NEAGU IBS PAVEL

A SCOTTISH ARTISTS WERE DISPLAYED RORY MCEWEN PAT DOUTHWAITE ALISTAIR PARK MICHAEL DOCHERTY

CORDELIA OLIVER ARTIST AND CRITIC

GEORGE OLIVER — SCOTTISH ARTIST-PHOTOGRAPHER

STEFAN WEWERKA   GUNTHER UECKER

LESLEY BEYNON - GALLERY ASSISTANT

GUNTHER UECKER AND STEFAN WERE TWO GERMAN ARTISTS EXHIBITING IN THE OFFICIAL EDINBURGH FESTIVAL EXHIBITION WITH THE PALINDROMIC TITLE OF
→ S T R A T E G Y — G E T — A R T S ←
THE TITLE WAS AN ARTWORK IN ITSELF BY THE SWISS ARTIST, ANDRE MONKINS → STRATEGY-GET-ARTS ← WAS PRESENTED AT EDINBURGH COLLEGE OF ART BECAUSE 35 ARTISTS WERE INVOLVED

Juuko Ikewada, the Japanese artist, and Ian Mackenzie Smith showed how two exhibitions of paintings could be utterly different in form and content. The sculpture of the Colombian Edgar Negret was the first of its kind to be shown in Scotland. It introduced the abstract, non-reflective painted metal forms which were in 1968 to win him the Sculpture Prize of the Venice Biennale under the aegis of the gallery. Nigerian artists from Oshogbo and mirror collages by John Eaves were two exhibitions which rose directly out of Richard Demarco's policy as director of the Traverse Gallery.

A lecture programme was initiated to enable artists to talk about their insights into the art world of London, New York and Buenos Aires. In March, the Gallery's first major exhibition of an entire national school was presented with the collaboration of Palma Buccarelli, the Director of The Museum of Modern Art in Rome. Art objects stretching to the limit long held definitions of painting and sculpture were shown, representing artists as historically important as Piero Manzoni, Jannis Kounellis, Pino Pascali, Alberto Burri and Lucio Fontana.

The exhibition should have had the international spotlight of the Festival.

In July, the entire gallery was given over to Patrick Heron's retrospective, his first on this scale in Britain. The Festival Fringe Exhibition flooded out from the Gallery into the Art College and even onto the roof garden of Goldberg's store, emphasising the Gallery's policy to extend its space to attract the widest possible public. William Crozier and James Howie were shown in the company of artists associated with Annely Juda's Hamilton Gallery.

The official Festival Programme was enhanced by the gallery's first major national undertaking the 'Edinburgh Open One Hundred'. It created the precedent of being the first 'open' exhibition devoted to contemporary British art to be seen in Scotland.

A great controversy which raged in the columns of the *Scotsman* was started by outraged Scots who considered Robyn Denny, John Hoyland, and Victor Newsome as unworthy of the three major £1000 prizes.

The autumn saw the first exhibition of fifteen contemporary Polish painters in Scotland. This was followed by a John Piper retrospective which occupied the entire gallery and a Christmas Exhibition which included the work of Aurelia Muñoz, Spain's most talented tapestry artist.

IT WAS AT LIBERTON
HOUSE THAT
THE TRAVERSE
THEATRE'S BLACK AND
WHITE BALL WAS INSPIRED
AND PLANNED BY PAMELA CURRIE

JAMES AND PAMELA CURRIE
WITH THEIR SONS PIERS AND ALASTAIR
AT LIBERTON HOUSE, EDINBURGH

Richard Demarco 1964

The year opened with a welcome to a new generation of Scottish artists, the Young Contemporaries. This exhibition compared well with the exhibition which followed of their Brazilian counterparts straight from the Paris Biennale des Jeunes.

In February, the gallery also presented its first Polish artist with the tapestries of Tamara Hans-Jaworska. Spring brought an attempt to redefine 'Aspects of Scottish Painting', outside the context of the usual exhibition outlet of the Royal Scottish Academy.

The first summer exhibition brought together the work of two artists, a Scot and an Englishman, Rory McEwen and Alan Wood, who displayed joyful inspiration through their skillful use of natural kinetic effects of light and movement in elements of landscape.

In June, Alan Davie's first major retrospective in his native land filled up every exhibition space in the gallery. This was presented in association with Gimpel Fils.

The official programme of the Festival welcomed the exhibition entitled 'Canada 101' – twenty-two Canadian artists, the result of my tour of Canada as guest of the Canada Council.

This was a follow-up to the 'Open 100'. Running concurrently at the gallery, at Hopetoun House (in the mansion and in the spacious grounds), in the North British Hotel, and in Goldberg's Store, the work of 133 artists was exhibited as part of the Festival Fringe Programme. This included thirty artists from the Denise Rene Gallery.

After the gallery had introduced a group exhibition of contemporary artists to Linlithgow in October, it completed the year's exhibition programme with four shows of Scottish figurative landscape painters: Lord Haig, James Morrison, Alexander Cree and Bet Low, contrasting with the abstract painting of their fellow Scot James Gavin and the English painter Paul Feiler, and the concrete poetry of Polish artist Franciszka Themerson.

Richard Demarco Gallery 1966-76: 1968

NEIL DALLAS BROWN IN HIS NEWPORT-ON-TAY STUDIO - FIFE

WILL MACLEAN IN HIS GATTESLID SCHOOLHOUSE STUDIO - FIFE

JAMES HOWIE IN HIS ARBROATH STUDIO

ROBERT CARGILL IN HIS ARBROATH STUDIO

RICHARD DEMARCO STUDIO 4 FEBRUARY 1975

VISITS TO THE STUDIO OF SIX SCOTTISH ARTISTS PRIOR TO THEIR EXHIBITION AT THE SALTIRE SOCIETY IN THE LAWNMARKET EDINBURGH

AN EXHIBITION ABOUT ARTISTS WHO HAVE BROUGHT CREATIVE IMAGINATIONS TO BEAR ON A BACKGROUND OF LIVING ON OR NEAR THE COAST.

DENNIS BUCHAN IN HIS ARBROATH STUDIO

FRED STIVEN IN HIS ABERDEEN STUDIO

The year began, as had 1968, with a welcome to the Scottish Young Contemporaries. This was followed by two exhibitions which introduced aspects of two national schools into Scotland.

The April retrospective exhibition of the Australian painter Arthur Boyd proved to be among the most popular and successful ever presented by the Gallery – a joyous hymn of praise to the art of applying oil paint to canvas to express highly emotional images on Biblical themes in the unlikely landscape of the Australian hinterland.

In what was an immensely rich and varied year, there followed a 'New Tendencies' exhibition of Scottish art which was one of five which emphasized the need to place young Scottish artists into a context other than that of the exhibition rooms of the Royal Scottish Academy. Michael Tyzack, Bill Featherston, Robert Downing, Robert Wise, Michael Roschlau and Yago Pericot vigorously expressed some new aspects of contemporary art from countries as far distant from each other as Canada, Germany, Spain, and England. All were related to a wide range of artists from Scotland. These included Fred Stiven with his box constructions, concrete poetry by Ian Hamilton Finlay and the powerful expressionist figure paintings of Pat Douthwaite, balanced by the comforting watercolour landscapes of George Mackie and the elegant abstracts of Robert Stewart, which hinted at the dramatic Loch Striven landscape he enjoys from his studio windows.

The Festival Exhibition at the gallery underlined the theme that a wide range of artistic expression was then relevant in Britain. The gallery was enhanced by Rory McEwen's sculpture environment 'The Tweed Road'. It literally filled one of the main exhibition rooms with an undulating tweed-covered form redolent with memories of Scottish highland roads.

The gallery presented both during and before the Festival a full programme of performance events, from another festival revue by Clive James and Tony Buffery, Lindsay Kemp's *White Pantomime,* and Geoff Moore's modern dance company *Moving Being,* to Nancy Cole's one-woman show on Gertrude Stein and the extraordinary Pakistani raga music of Salamat and Nazakat Ali Khan and the unique entertainment of John McGrath, John Gorman and Mike McGear in *The Scaffold.*

Richard Demarco Gallery 1966-76: 1969

TRAVERSE THEATRE

JAMES CLOSE ~ THE HOME OF
THE ORIGINAL TRAVERSE THEATRE

Richard Demarco 9?

In January, I was invited by the United States Government to tour American art centres. The first four months saw exhibitions of artists new to Scotland – Peter Lloyd Jones, Norman Adams, Margot Perryman and Margaret Mellis.

In March the Three Arts Ball was held in Edinburgh's Assembly Rooms in aid of the Traverse, Ledlanet and the gallery, and Nancy Meckler's experimental company 'The Freehold' gave devastating performances of *Antigone,* with outstanding performances from Dinah Starr and Stephen Rea.

A first-ever exhibition of Maltese artists in Scotland was followed in June by Trevor Bell's large kite-like paintings which dominated the whole gallery.

Next an all-Australian show contrasted the established masters Arthur Boyd and Sydney Nolan with two younger artists Leonard Hessing and Robert Owen working in acrylic, aluminium, and other materials.

The outstanding event of the year was 'Strategy: Get Arts' which for the first time gave the official Edinburgh Festival programme a truly contemporary art exhibition.

At the gallery the work of four Scots – Alistair Park, Rory McEwen, Michael Docherty and Pat Douthwaite – and three Romanians, Paul Neagu, Horea Bernea and Pavel Ilie – indicated some 'New Directions'.

In the autumn Lowe Donald of Peebles commissioned four artists to express their ideas in tweed. In October the paintings of two English artists, Bryan Senior and Patrick Hayman, were shown with the work of two Scots, William MacLean and Tony Valentine.

In December, Gerald Laing and Andrew Mylius were shown, with Buttercup Garrad.

Richard Demarco Gallery 1966-76: 1970

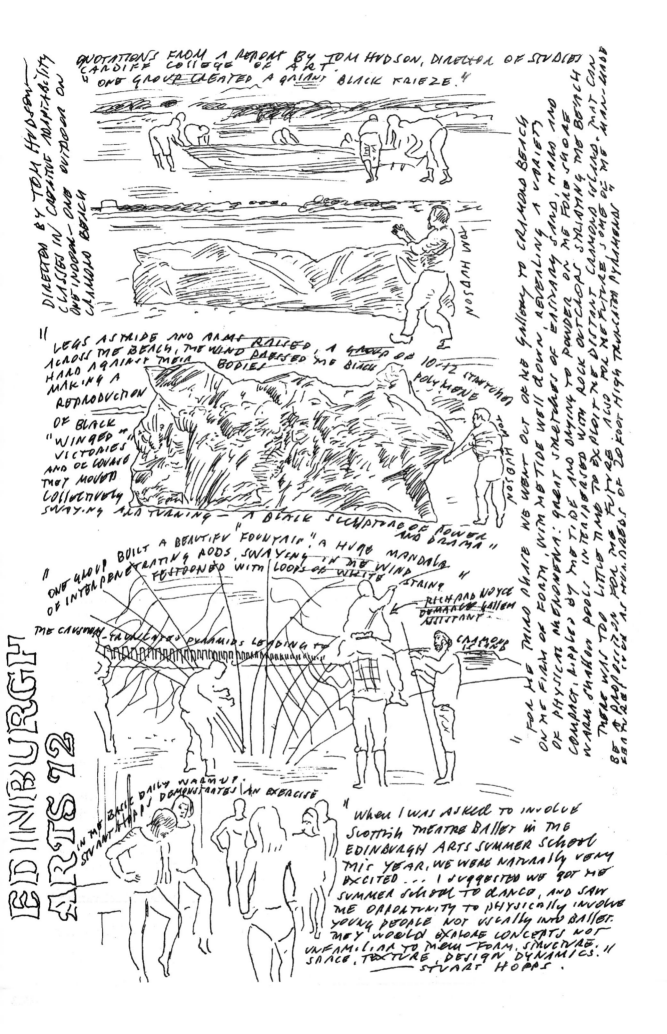

QUOTATIONS FROM A REPORT BY TOM HUDSON, DIRECTOR OF STUDIES CARDIFF COLLEGE OF ART.

"ONE GROUP CREATED A GIANT BLACK FRIEZE."

DIRECTED BY TOM HUDSON. CLASSES IN CREATIVE ADAPTABILITY ONE INDOOR—ONE OUTDOOR ON CRAMOND BEACH

"LEGS ASTRIDE AND ARMS RAISED, A GROUP OF 10+12 STRETCHED ACROSS THE BEACH, THE WIND PRESSED THE BLACK POLYTHENE HARD AGAINST THEIR BODIES MAKING A REPRODUCTION OF BLACK "WINGED" VICTORIES AND OF COURSE THEY MOVED COLLECTIVELY SWAYING AND TURNING — A BLACK SCULPTURE OF POWER AND DRAMA"

TOM HUDSON

"ONE GROUP BUILT A BEAUTIFUL "FOUNTAIN". A HUGE MANDALA OF INTERPENETRATING RODS, SWAYING IN THE WIND FESTOONED WITH LOOPS OF WHITE STRING"

THE CAUSEWAY—TRUNCATED PYRAMIDS LEADING TO CRAMOND ISLAND

RICHARD NOYCE DUMFRIES GALLERY ASSISTANT

CRAMOND ISLAND

"FOR THE THIRD PHASE WE WENT OUT OF THE GALLERY TO CRAMOND BEACH ON THE FILM OF FORM, WITH THE TIDE WELL DOWN, REVEALING A VARIETY OF PHYSICAL PHENOMENA: GREAT STRETCHES OF EASHARD SAND, MUD AND COMPACT, RIPPLED BY THE TIDE AND DRYING TO POWDER ON THE FORESHORE WARM SHALLOW POOLS INTERLACED WITH ROCK OUTCROPS SHELVING THE BEACH THERE WAS TOO LITTLE TIME TO EXPLOIT THE DISTANT CRAMOND ISLAND THAT CAN BE REACHED ON FOOT ... ALSO FOR THE FUTURE SOME OF THE MAN-MADE FEATURES OF COMPOSITION SUCH AS HUGE SHEDS OF 20 FOOT HIGH TRUNCATED PYRAMIDS"

EDINBURGH ARTS 72

IN THE BASIC DAILY WARMUP, STUART HOPPS DEMONSTRATES AN EXERCISE

"WHEN I WAS ASKED TO INVOLVE SCOTTISH THEATRE BALLET IN THE EDINBURGH ARTS SUMMER SCHOOL THIS YEAR, WE WERE NATURALLY VERY EXCITED ... I SUGGESTED WE GOT THE SUMMER SCHOOL TO DANCE, AND SAW THE OPPORTUNITY TO PHYSICALLY INVOLVE YOUNG PEOPLE NOT USUALLY INTO BALLET. THEY WOULD EXPLORE CONCEPTS NOT UNFAMILIAR TO THEM — FORM, STRUCTURE, SPACE, TEXTURE, DESIGN DYNAMICS."
— STUART HOPPS.

The year began with four one-man shows which related the process of oil painting to a total environment by the Chinese artist Li Yuan Chia and the wall-hung objects of Michael Craig-Martin, suggesting the growing importance of the conceptual art attitudes of the seventies.

Once again a Scottish artist, Gordon Bryce, was seen in an international context, his paintings contrasting with the strangely grotesque series of monochromatic figure painting by the Australian painter Philippe Mora. At the same time Paul Neagu and Horia Bernea were being introduced to London in collaboration with the Sigi Krauss Gallery.

In February the entire gallery was devoted to paintings by the American artist, Jon Schueler, inspired by the skies above the Sound of Sleat. Fleur Cowles was, like Jon Schueler, given the entire gallery space in June to relate her own paintings to her international art collection.

Altogether, including the January exhibition, the gallery presented thirty-three one-man shows, thirteen of which were by Scottish artists.

William McCance's posthumous exhibition was unique as it was the first devoted to his work. He was given little credit in his life for his experiments as a cubist painter.

Hamish Fulton's exhibition introduced the language of 'land art' into Scotland with the photographic evidence he made of journeys into poetic Northern European landscapes.

The work of Shirtsleeve Studio revealed the full sophisticated, clever and often humorous imagery of London's most successful husband and wife graphic art team, Nancy Fouts and Malcolm Fowler.

Four printmakers, two Englishmen, Norman Ackroyd and Michael Peel, the American Ed Ruscha, and the German Stefan Wewerka, revealed how prints can be made from the most diverse techniques and subject matter.

Ian Hamilton Finlay's one-man show proved how a fusion of neon-lit sculptural forms and his unique language of *poésie concrète* could result in an art experience the form of which should inspire the designers of commercial neon signs to employ artists of such sensitivity.

The Edinburgh Festival Exhibition was at the gallery, its first use as an official festival venue, and introduced contemporary Romanian Art to Britain – the result of three years negotiations between the gallery and the Romanian National Union of Artists, involving me in three visits to Romania as the guest of the Union.

Richard Demarco Gallery 1966-76: 1971

GALERIA

THE BASIC TASK OF THE GALLERY AS DEFINED IN THE CATALOGUE OF THE DEMARCO GALLERY'S 1979 EDINBURGH FESTIVAL EXHIBITION "—THE GALLERY, AS A NON COMMERCIAL INSTITUTION WITH RATHER THIN RELATIONSHIPS WITH THE OUTER INSTITUTIONAL WORLD WORKS WITHOUT ANY GAINS IN TERMS OF MONEY OR PRESTIGE"

FOKSAL PSP

THE GALLERY'S MAIN TASK, WHICH IT TAKES UP AND PURPORTS TO FULFILL, IS IMPOSED ON IT BY THE CONDITIONS PREVAILING IN MODERN ART AND SOCIETY IN WHICH IT IS SUBMERGED. THE BASIC TASK HAS NOT BEEN OUTLINED OR PROGRAMMED IN ANY DETAIL. IT IS A CULTURAL TASK THAT MUST BE CARRIED OUT IN PRACTICE ALONGSIDE DEVELOPING EVENTS AND IN TIMES WHICH CAN SCARCELY BE PREDICTED.

TADEUSZ KANTOR

MARIA STANGRET

WIESLAW BOROWSKI THE DIRECTOR OF THE FOKSAL

HENRYK STASEWSKI FRIEND OF MALEVICH

EDWARD KRASINSKI

I WONDER HOW THE SCOTTISH ART COUNCIL COULD ACCEPT IT'S

THE DEMARCO GALLERY WAS PLEASED TO INTRODUCE THE FOLLOWING ARTISTS TO THE FOKSAL GALLERY; TIM MACMILLAC AND DAVID MACH (FROM SCOTLAND)

AN ARCHITECT (FROM ENGLAND) ROYDEN RABINOWITCH (FROM CANADA)

THE FOKSAL GALLERY WORKS CLOSELY WITH THE MUSEUM OF BALTIM NOW AS PART OF THE MUSEUM SZTUKI IN LODZ.

THIS WORK WAS INTRODUCED INTO BRITAIN IN 1979 BY THE DEMARCO GALLERY AS PART OF THE 1979 EDINBURGH FESTIVAL.

THE FOKSAL GALLERY WAS FOUNDED, LIKE THE DEMARCO GALLERY IN 1966, AND LIKE THE DEMARCO GALLERY IT HAS RESOLUTELY DEFENDED THE IDEA OF INTERNATIONALISM IN THE CONTEMPORARY VISUAL ARTS

Much was to change in my attitude to the way in which the performing and visual arts could be intertwined when I saw for the first time the Cricot 2 Theatre in action when they appeared in Paris with their production of Witkiewicz's *Les Cordonniers.*

Sean Connery invited me to become the first director of the Scottish International Education Trust with the trust's office located on the top floor of 8 Melville Crescent.

The first version of 'Edinburgh Arts' extended from July 3 to 28. It provided a pre-Festival exhibition by sixteen artists, including the Scots James Barclay, Michael Docherty, and John Knox in relation to such Americans as Tom Ockerse, John Schueler and Rick Harder.

Tom Hudson directed a most effective experimental sculpture workshop on Cramond beach and Stuart Hopps extended the concept of dance into every conceivable space at Melville Crescent, both inside and outside the gallery.

The Los Angeles artist David Helder created, with the help of twenty-five fellow participants, a 'land art drawing' upon the green grassy crater slopes of Arthur's Seat's extinct volcano. His fellow artists, wearing red fluorescent jackets, recreated fleetingly the forms of Edinburgh townscape upon this immense green mountainous space which dominates Edinburgh's city centre.

Richard Noyce and Ian Ledward produced a wind sculpture which captured the music of the sea breezes on Cramond beach.

All of this gave impetus to the 1972 Festival Exhibition of 'land art' sculpture by South African artists, Kevin Atkinson, Richard Wake, and Dimitri Nicolas-Fanourakis in the parkland of Hopetoun House.

As part of the official Festival programme contemporary art of Poland was presented through the work of forty-two artists and Tadeusz Kantor's Cricot 2 production of *The Water Hen* which equalled in intensity the images created by Joseph Beuys' 72-hour-long 1970 concert, *Celtic Kinloch-Rannoch,* the exhibition was made possible by the support of the Scottish International Education Trust.

In October there was a one woman exhibition of the overwhelming tormented surreal figures of Pat Douthwaite, and Michael Horowitz revealed his passionate concern for the culture found around the football club Wolverhampton Wanderers. Coinciding with this the gallery staff played the Arts Council at football and lost four goals to one!

The year ended in November and December with two exhibitions of paintings which placed Bill Gillon, Ainslie Yule, John Busby, as Scottish artists beside the work of Roy Johnston from Belfast and Derek Hyatt from Yorkshire.

'Maps and map-making' represented the world of John Bartholomew and Son, cartographers. This exhibition fitted remarkably well with the graphic art of an extraordinary artist – twelve-year-old Polly Donnison, who senses even more than G.K. Chesterton the importance of the world of fairy-tales. Jeff Cloves and Robert Bradford extended ideas of visual art 'actions' with poetry and song.

Richard Demarco Gallery 1966-76: 1972

THE DEMARCO GALLERY HAD TO LOOK TOWARDS EAST EUROPEAN
COUNTRIES PARTICULARLY TO POLAND AND ROMANIA AS WELL AS
TO GERMANY AND ITALY WHERE THE WORLD OF GABRIELLA CARDAZZO
AT THE GALLERIA del CAVALLINO
IN VENICE PROVIDED AN INSPIRATION
THE CAVALLINO HAD BEEN FOUNDED
BY GABRIELLA'S FATHER IN VENICE
IN 1943. FROM ITS VERY
BEGINNINGS IT DEFENDED THE
INTERNATIONAL AVANT GARDE
DESPITE THE AGONIES OF WAR-TORN
ITALY. SOON THE NAMES OF
JACKSON POLLOCK AND SAMUEL
BECKETT WERE IDENTIFIED WITH
ITS NAME AS A GALLERY AND
PUBLISHING HOUSE.

GABRIELLA AND HER BROTHER
PAOLO CONTINUED THE
GALLERY'S COMMITMENT TO
INTERNATIONALISM AND
IT SEEMED INEVITABLE
THAT THE CAVALLINO
AND THE DEMARCO
GALLERIES SHOULD
COLLABORATE TO
BRING THE SPIRIT OF
THE EDINBURGH ARTS
JOURNEYS TO ITALY.

THE TOWER OF ST. RULE DOMINATES THE
RUINS OF ST. ANDREWS CATHEDRAL. A GUIDE
FOR THOSE WHO SEEK TO KNOW WHAT PLACE OF
RELIGIOUS WORSHIP STOOD HERE BEFORE THE
CHRISTIAN ERA

GABRIELLA CARDAZZO
WALKING ALONG THE ST. ANDREWS
HARBOUR WALL
ACCOMPANYING
HER FELLOW EDINBURGH ARTS '76
PARTICIPANTS
FOCUSSING THEIR
THOUGHTS ON A
VOYAGE TOWARDS
THE BALTIC.

ST. ANDREWS, THE MEDIEVAL
HARBOUR — A PLACE WHERE
GENERATIONS OF MEDIEVAL
UNIVERSITY STUDENTS COULD
CONTEMPLATE THE JOURNEY
WHICH LINKED THEM TO
THE GREAT EUROPEAN CENTRES
OF LEARNING AS FAR DISTANT
AS OXFORD CAMBRIDGE, PARIS
AND BOLOGNA & VENICE

BECAUSE OF THE EDINBURGH ARTS JOURNEYS VENETIAN ARTISTS
SUCH AS PAOLO PATELLI GUIDO SARTORELLI. ANSELMO ANSELMI
PICCOLO SILLANI, ALBERTO VARISCO, PEGGY STUFFI FOUND THEMSELVES
EXPLORING THE ROAD TO MEIKLE SEGGIE WEST TO THE HEBRIDES AND
NORTH TO THE ORKNEYS VIA MALTA, SARDINIA. CORSICA CROATIA. SLOVENIA
AND BOSNIA.

    "THE JOURNEY WITHIN OURSELVES HAS BEGUN DISCOVERY BECOMES
PART OF OUR DAILY LIFE, PEOPLE APPEAR AND DISAPPEAR EVERY DAY
AS IN A DREAM SOMETIMES ONLY A NAME AND A FADED IMAGE
REMAIN ON OUR MEMORY. PLACES AND TEMPLES ARE PRETEXTS TO JOIN
ALL TOGETHER. WE TRAVEL FOR MILES AND MILES TO REACH OUR GOALS WHICH
ARE SO DIFFERENT AND SO SIMILAR ONE FROM ANOTHER "
                    GABRIELLA CARDAZZO — VENICE 21 July '76

The Edinburgh Arts 73 project lasted six weeks, starting in August and incorporating the three weeks of the Festival. Over 100 participating artists and students benefited from the Cricot 2 Theatre's presentation of *Lovelies and Dowdies* and Tadeusz Kantor's master classes on his work as a visual artist and on his Cricot philosophy.

Joseph Beuys gave his non-stop 12 hour lecture. Inspired by the writings of Anacharsis Cloots in relation to the French Revolution, this was a piece of sculpture where school blackboards could be seen to be the ideal surface for the drawings and diagrams he chose to illustrate his philosophy on art education, interdisciplinary research and communication.

The Edinburgh Festival Exhibition introduced contemporary Austrian art to Britain.

The overwhelming expressionistic language of Austrian art was expressed through Arnulf Rainer's performance/drawings and the sculptures of Anton Christian, Bruno Gironcoli and Mario Terzic. Gunter Brus, Peter Wiebel and Valie Export revealed how performance art is a natural language for Austrian artists.

This exhibition was near in its ritualistic imagery to the actions and performances of the Yugoslav artists Marina Abramovic, Rasa Todosijevic and Zoran Popovic.

The seven Parisian artists Piotr Kowalski, Christian Boltanski, Wolfgang Gafgen, Gerard Gasiorowski, Jean Le Gac, Etienne Martin, Gerard Titus-Carmel and Vladimir Velickovic presented a cooler, more intellectually sophisticated French concern for the visual reality recalling the concerns of Proust, Cézanne and Marcel Duchamp.

The year ended, with what was to prove to be a historic exhibition – that of four Galleria del Cavallino artists from Venice: Romano Perusini, Franco Costalonga, Anselmo Anselmi and Paolo Patelii.

It marked the beginning of the vital dialogue between myself and Gabriella Cardazzo as gallery directors identified with two cities not formerly linked on the map of the international art world – Venice and Edinburgh.

Richard Demarco Gallery 1966-76: 1973

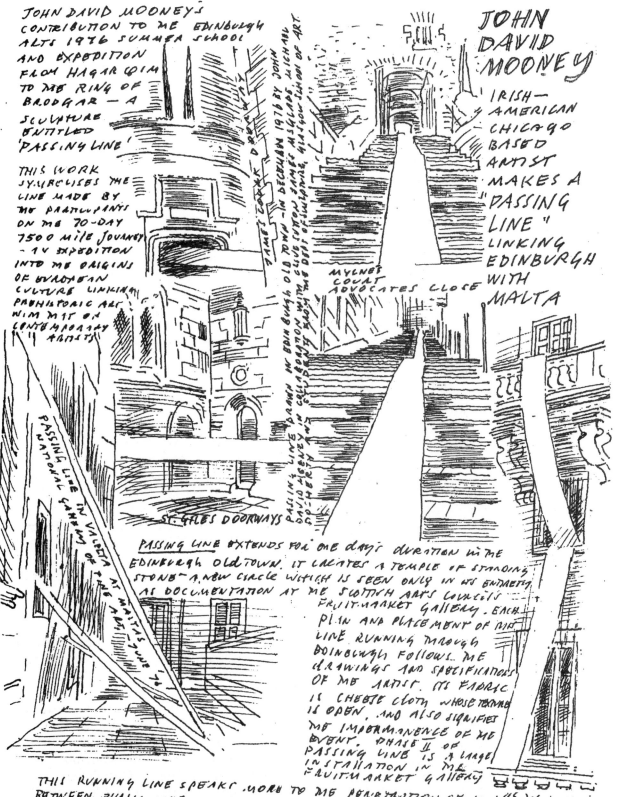

JOHN DAVID MOONEY'S CONTRIBUTION TO THE EDINBURGH ARTS 1976 SUMMER SCHOOL AND EXPEDITION FROM HAGAR QIM TO THE RING OF BRODGAR — A SCULPTURE ENTITLED 'PASSING LINE'

THIS WORK SYMBOLISES THE LINE MADE BY THE PARTICIPANTS ON THE 70-DAY 7500 MILE JOURNEY — AN EXPEDITION INTO THE ORIGINS OF EUROPEAN CULTURE LINKING PREHISTORIC ART WITH THAT OF CONTEMPORARY ARTISTS

JAMES' COURT DOORWAY — PASSING LINE DRAWN IN EDINBURGH OLD TOWN IN DECEMBER 1976 BY JOHN DAVID MOONEY IN COLLABORATION WITH CLIFF CUTLER JAMES HASLAM MICHAEL DOHERTY AND STUDENTS FROM THE DEPT OF SCULPTURE, GLASGOW SCHOOL OF ART

MYLNE'S COURT ADVOCATES CLOSE

ST. GILES DOORWAYS

PASSING LINE IN VALETTA AT MALTA'S NATIONAL GALLERY OF THE ARTS JUNE 76

JOHN DAVID MOONEY

IRISH — AMERICAN CHICAGO BASED ARTIST MAKES A "PASSING LINE" LINKING EDINBURGH WITH MALTA

PASSING LINE EXTENDS FOR ONE DAY'S DURATION IN THE EDINBURGH OLD TOWN. IT CREATES A TEMPLE OF STANDING STONE — A NEW CIRCLE WHICH IS SEEN ONLY IN ITS ENTIRETY AS DOCUMENTATION AT THE SCOTTISH ARTS COUNCIL'S FRUITMARKET GALLERY. EACH PLAN AND PLACEMENT OF THE LINE RUNNING THROUGH EDINBURGH FOLLOWS THE DRAWINGS AND SPECIFICATIONS OF THE ARTIST. ITS FABRIC IS CHEESE CLOTH WHOSE TEXTURE IS OPEN, AND ALSO SIGNIFIES THE IMPERMANENCE OF THE EVENT. PHASE II OF PASSING LINE IS A LARGE INSTALLATION IN THE FRUITMARKET GALLERY

THIS RUNNING LINE SPEAKS MORE TO THE PENETRATION OF WALLS AND OPENINGS BETWEEN PUBLIC LIFE AND PRIVATE LIFE, BETWEEN LIGHT AND DARK, AND BETWEEN TYING THE KNOWN TO THE UNKNOWN. THE INFINITE EXTENSIONS OF THE METAPHYSICAL CONTEXT OF THIS LINE WEAVING IN TIME AND SPACE ARE THE BODY OF THIS WORK. IT IS NOT A PERMANENT PIECE, IT IS FLEETING. IT IS INSTALLED FOR ONE DAY — — — SITES CHOSEN THROUGH WHICH THIS LINE PASSES RELATE TO THE PLAN OF HAGAR QIM, ENLARGED AND INTERPOSED OVER THE CITY OF EDINBURGH " — JOHN DAVID MOONEY — CHICAGO OCT 76

This was to be a momentous year with many new sources of energy revealed to offset the sad event of the gallery moving from its Melville Crescent premises to the temporary basement office accommodation in Great King Street. By this time six long-standing members of the Board of Directors – Andrew Elliott, John Martin, James Walker, Mark Goldberg, Vivien Gough-Cooper and Lillian Hope Collins – had retired.

The January exhibition was essentially about sculpture though it included the Bostonian painter, Earl Powell. Ovidiu Maitec was welcomed back after his successful introduction into Britain at the gallery's 1971 Festival Exhibition. His work is in the best tradition of carved wood sculpture originating in Romanian iconography. Nigel Hall managed to prove that memorable sculptural images could be established with wall-suspended metal lines. Nigel Van Wieck offered an indoor environment of neon-lit perspex forms.

Whilst I was involved in a lecture tour of New England from Washington to Boston, the gallery's exhibition programme at Melville Crescent was concluded with an exhibition of four sculptors – Julian Snelling, with his quirky kinetic small-scale wooden objects hinted playfully at an erotic symbolism; Richard England also used wood to make what were essentially macquettes for a contemporary version of Mediterranean temples built for long forgotten religious rituals; Alice Beberman created an environment for her crocheted almost full size figures; Angelo Bozzolla's work questioned deeper the meaning of sculpture, although his work was defined as a frieze, a book, and a tape; it was sculpture in essence.

Thus the last two exhibitions at Melville Crescent defined the widest possible range of contemporary language now used by the sculptors. They were a comment on the inadequacy of the space which most art galleries now provide. On March 10 there was a party to celebrate the gallery's years at Melville Crescent. Frank Ashton-Gwatkin was among the many friends of the gallery who travelled far to attend this cheerful occasion.

The highlight in March was the gallery's showing at the ICA London of the film, directed by Ken McMullen, of *Lovelies and Dowdies*. Over 150 of the gallery's London friends supported this event. I had to make another tour of the States from May 4-17 and returned to organize an exhibition at the Museum of Modern Art, Oxford of Edinburgh Arts 73 documentation, mainly in the form of photographs and slides. At the same time, I also presented a Joseph Beuys 'event' at Forrest Hill entitled, 'Three Pots Action'.

It was an act of homage to the gallery's space which now existed outside the white, cube-like rooms of Melville Crescent.

On July 11 I was surprised to be invited for the first time to the Special Unit of HM Prison, Barlinnie. It was the beginning of his dialogue with Jimmy Boyle as an artist and Larry Winters as a poet.

Richard Demarco Gallery 1966-76: 1974

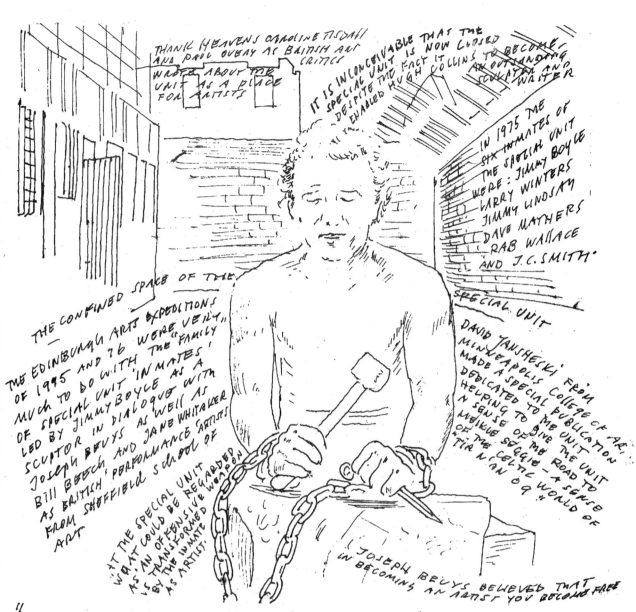

THANK HEAVENS CAROLINE TISDALL AND PAUL OVERY AS BRITISH ART CRITICS WROTE ABOUT THE UNIT AS A PLACE FOR ARTISTS

IT IS INCONCEIVABLE THAT THE SPECIAL UNIT IS NOW CLOSED DESPITE THE FACT THAT IT ENABLED HUGH COLLINS TO BECOME AN OUTSTANDING SCULPTOR AND WRITER

IN 1975 THE SIX INMATES OF THE SPECIAL UNIT WERE : JIMMY BOYLE LARRY WINTERS JIMMY LINDSAY DAVE MATHERS RAB WALLACE AND J.C. SMITH.

THE CONFINED SPACE OF THE SPECIAL UNIT

THE EDINBURGH ARTS EXPEDITIONS OF 1975 AND 76 WERE VERY MUCH TO DO WITH THE "FAMILY" OF SPECIAL UNIT 'INMATES' LED BY JIMMY BOYCE AS A SCUPTOR IN DIALOGUE WITH JOSEPH BEUYS AS WELL AS BILL BEECH AND JANE WHITAKER AS BRITISH PERFORMANCE ARTISTS FROM SHEFFIELD SCHOOL OF ART

AT THE SPECIAL UNIT WHAT COULD BE REGARDED AS AN OFFENSIVE WEAPON IS TRANSFORMED BY THE INMATE AS ARTIST.

DAVID JANSHESKI FROM MINNEAPOLIS COLLEGE OF ART MADE A SPECIAL PUBLICATION DEDICATED TO THE UNIT HELPING TO GIVE THE UNIT IN SENSE OF THE "ROAD TO WEMBLEY" - A SENSE OF THE CELTIC - 4 WORLD OF TIR NAN OG

(JOSEPH BEUYS BELIEVED THAT IN BECOMING AN ARTIST YOU BECOME FREE

THE JOURNEY THAT THE EDINBURGH ARTS GROUP WERE ABOUT TO EMBARK ON WAS SHROUDED IN A MIST OF HIDDEN QUALITIES THAT EMBRACE TIME, SPACE ART AND SOCIETY, EACH OF WHICH MUST BE CLARIFIED IN RELATION TO PEOPLE AND THIS WAS THE SALIENT POINT OF THE EXERCISE — PEOPLE. BY DESIGN THE GROUP SET OUT FROM AN AREA THAT WAS A SUPERSTRUCTURE OF MODERN TECHNOLOGY CONTAINING ELECTRONIC EYES. BARBED WIRE, RADAR EQUIPMENT ALL SURROUNDED BY HUGE WALLS. THIS SPACE IS A MONUMENT TO SOCIETY'S FAILURE TO MAKE POSITIVE SOCIAL ADVANCES, THE ANTITHESIS OF THE MONUMENTS OF CALLANISH WHERE THE GROUP WERE HEADING. WITHIN THE HUGE WALLS THERE IS CONTAINED A MINUTE SAMPLE OF SOCIETY — SIX MEN — WHO ARE SO PHYSICALLY RESTRICTED THAT THEIR TOTAL SPACE IS A FEW STEPS IN ANY GIVEN DIRECTION. THE JOURNEY IS SIGNIFICANT IN THAT IT DEFINED UNEQUIVOCALLY THE RESTRICTIONS OF CERTAIN "CIVILISED" DWELT-IN SPACES IN RELATION TO THOSE UNINHABITED. AS THE TWO GROUPS PARTED WITHIN THE WALLS, THE EDINBURGH ARTS GROUP WALKED THROUGH ALL THE ELECTRONIC DEVICES UNFETTERED. COMMUNICATION WAS THEN TO BE THE LINK BETWEEN BOTH PARTIES, THE ONE WALKING, DRIVING TO THE FAR NORTH OF SCOTLAND, THROUGH SOME OF THE MOST BEAUTIFUL COUNTRYSIDE IN THE WORLD, THE OTHER PACING, COLLIDING, CLASHING WITHIN THE SMALL AREA. TIMES WERE MADE FOR CORRESPONDENCE EACH DAY ... THE MAIL FLOWED IN ABUNDANCE EITHER WAY ... IT WAS A SEARCH FOR TRUTH AND BEAUTY — A CATHARSIS OF THE PRESENT AND A RETURN TO THE PAST TO FIND IT.
THE ABOVE STATEMENT BY JIMMY BOYLE WAS PART OF HIS CONTRIBUTION TO THE 1976 EDINBURGH ARTS CATALOGUE.

The 1974 Festival programme contained a record number of exhibitions.

Jimmy Boyle's sculptures were shown at 142 High Street, beside the poetry of another inmate of the Special Unit – Larry Winters and the work of inmates of other prisons.

At the Bank of Scotland, St. Andrews Square there was an exhibition by staff and post-graduate students of the Department of Sculpture of Sheffield's Polytechnic College of Art, including Bryan MacDonald, the head of the department and his senior lecturer, Manuel Chetcuti.

Within the Victorian Baroque splendour of the Royal College of Physicians building in Queen Street, the artists of Galleria del Cavallino were presented, among them Paolo Patelii, Anselmi, Teardo, Legnaghi and Sutej.

In the same gallery were two exhibitions of American painting, one representing the Boston Visual Arts Union and the other the faculty and students of the post-graduate Hoffburger school of painting of the Maryland Institute of Art. The school, like the Boston Arts Union, represented unusual aspects of American contemporary art.

There was also an exhibition of Kansas City artists, including Tommy Gomersall, David Dunlap, Warren Rosser, Jim Sajovic and William Volkesz. At Hopetoun House, Jud Fine made an environment of broken glass and stones Paul Bowen and Jill Breakstone made an environment at Forrest Hill, John Paskiewicz impregnated the Forrest Hill walls with his large-sized xerox drawings.

At 142 High Street in collaboration with Anne Madden of ICI (Paints Division) six English artists showed what could be done using white Vymura paint with sculptural statements.

There was also a special programme of Festival lectures given by Sir Roland Penrose, Douglas Hall, Colin Thompson, Paolo Soleri and Norbert Lynton. These lectures were presented at the same time as a programme of music recitals which enabled Leonard Friedman, Kenneth Van Barthold and Dr. Peter Williams to talk about music in relation to the musical instruments they played.

The high point of the gallery's Festival activities was the Conference on Scottish Oil held not inappropriately at the Poorhouse.

The conference was fortunate to involve such as Buckminster Fuller, Joseph Beuys, Herman Swart, the Dutch art critic, Dr Gavin Strang, Peter Cook, Alex Fletcher, Fr Anthony Ross, Alvin Boyarsky, Director of the Architectural Association, and Owen Dudley Edwards acting as chairman, Lord Bute, Prof Barrie Wilson and Dr John Francis were among the organising committee and Gerald Laing, Michael Spens and Magdalena Abakanowicz.

The Chicago sculptor Phil Hitchcock presented his action 'A Rat Trap' which posed this fitting question: is the contemporary artist only tap-dancing in an empty room?

Doug Hales, Michael Meyers, Steven Whitacre and Dan Lowenstein presented or participated in three other actions. Paul Neagu collaborating with Paul Hitchcock and Jud Fine presented previews of his *Going Tornado* performances. Jack Lansley and Sally Porter directed with great vigour the Edinburgh Arts Dance Workshop to present a memorable event at Lochgilphead which made special comment on the danger of pollution from unrestricted development of oil and tourism.

Richard Demarco Gallery 1966-76: 1974

JOSEPH BEUYS HAD GIVEN ME FAIR WARNING. "IF I COME TO
EDINBURGH AND WE WORK TOGETHER YOUR GALLERY WILL NO
LONGER BE ABLE TO JUSTIFY ITSELF. IT WILL HAVE TO CHANGE."

AND CHANGE IT DID THROUGH THE SPIRIT OF AVANT GARDISM BROUGHT
TO SCOTLAND THROUGH THE EXHIBITIONS: "STRATEGY-GET-ARTS" FROM
GERMANY. ROMANIAN ART TODAY AND THE ATELIER 72 EXHIBITION
FROM POLAND. THEY REPRESENTED A NEW WAY OF PRESENTING AND
MAKING ART. THEY WERE THE THREE OFFICIAL EDINBURGH FESTIVAL EXHIBITIONS
WHICH THE DEMARCO GALLERY PRESENTED FOR THE YEARS 1970, 71 AND 72.

ADDED TO THAT WAS THE EXPERIMENTAL NATURE OF THE DEMARCO
GALLERY'S INTERNATIONAL SUMMER SCHOOLS WITH JOSEPH BEUYS, TADEUSZ
KANTOR, FRANK ASHTON GWATKIN, HUGH MACDIARMID, BUCKMINSTER FULLER
MAGDALENA ABAKANOWICZ, PAUL NEAGU, GEORGE MELLY, PATRICK REYNTIENS
AMONG MANY OTHERS.

FAREWELL TO MELVILLE CRESCENT

MARKING THE VERY LAST DAY OF THE DEMARCO GALLERY'S LIFE
AT NUMBER 8 MELVILLE CRESCENT — 10TH MARCH 197
A PARTY WITH ENTERTAINMENT BY GUEST ARTISTS
INCLUDING LEONARD FRIEDMAN, ISLA ST CLAIR

N.W.M. BEETSON.

ANDREW ELLIOTT

JIMMY WALKER

JOHN MARTIN

TOGETHER THEY
FORMED THE ORIGINAL
FOUNDING BOARD
OF DEMARCO GALLERY
DIRECTORS

RICHARD ENGLAND

ISLA ST CLAIR - THE
SCOTTISH SINGER
OF FOLK SONGS
IN THE BUCHAN TRADITION

LORD HAIG — ARTIST
AT ONE TIME CHAIRMAN OF THE
FRIENDS OF THE DEMARCO GALLERY

FRANK ASHTON GWATKIN
DIPLOMAT - ART PATRON
NOVELIST (AUTHOR OF
KIMONO) AND
JOHN PARIS.
HE ENTERED THE
CONSULAR SERVICE IN 1913

DUNCAN MACFARLANE
GONE OF THE
DIRECTORS WHO
GALLERY DECIDED
HOUSE IN MONTEITH
ROYAL MILE

SALLY HOLMAN
EXHIBITION
DEMARCO
GALLERY

YVES WALKER

ANN MACFARLANE

THE FINAL EXHIBITION PRESENTED IN THE FORM OF 4 ONE-MAN SHOWS
SCULPTURE BY RICHARD ENGLAND AND JULIAN SNELLING — AND A DRAWING
TAPE AND BOOK INSTALLATION BY ANGELO BOZZOLA — AND ENVIRONMENTAL
SCULPTURE BY ALICE BEBERMAN — AS WELL AS WORK BY 8 AMERICAN
METALSMITHS AND JEWELLERS CO-ORDINATED BY BARBARA KRAN.

The year 1975 was an historical one, in which the gallery moved into new premises on Edinburgh's historic Royal Mile, to a building known as Monteith House, neatly wedged between Carrubers Close and John Knox's House, beside one of the few remaining medieval town water wells. Viewed from a certain angle the gallery's new street sign becomes one with the sign outside Carrubers Mission so it can be imagined that the two signs read as one, both with white lettering on black indicating "Jesus Saves – The Richard Demarco Gallery". The gallery must be benefiting from divine intervention of some kind to have survived the difficulties facing the British art world at this time of economical and spiritual crises.

Monteith House was opened on July 16 with two one-woman exhibitions, by the Yugoslav artist Jagoda Buic, whose tapestries are indeed soft, woven sculptures and the Canadian printmaker Pat Martin Bates, whose work explores the dissolution of matter.

April saw a major exhibition meriting the space of the Arts Council's Fruit Market Gallery and presenting 11 Scottish artists whose work is essentially sculptural despite the fact that some of them have established their reputations as painters.

This exhibition toured afterwards in England and Scotland, defining achievements of artists vital to the development of art language in Scotland.

Tam MacPhail made unexpectedly effective use of the iron girders supporting the Fruit Market roof and in so doing personified that kind of Scottish artist who questions the space of art galleries and who deserves to be seen in a context beyond that of the art world.

The 1975 Edinburgh Arts was part of the gallery's strategy to provide new spaces for such artists and depended strongly on the 'journey' it defined in two sections.

The first introduced the participating artists to the art worlds of Malta, Italy and Yugoslavia, and the second to Scotland and England with an emphasis on Sheffield, the Hebrides, Aberdeen and Edinburgh. Among the exhibitions and 'actions' presented were those of Anselmo Anselmi and Peggy Stuffi at the National Gallery, Malta, Bryan Macdonald and Paolo Patelli at Manikata Church, Malta and Barbara Koslowska and Zbigniew Makarewicz on the beaches of Malta and Lewis. Through creative use of the space offered in the catalogue Cioni Carpi, Jean Le Gac, Guiseppi Chiari contributed conceptual art pieces.

After the Festival the Arts Council's Fruit Market was again used for a major exhibition which introduced Yugoslav contemporary art through the work of 42 artists. Ida Baird, Marina Abramovic, Slobadan Dimitijevic, Goran Trbuljak all contributed 'actions'.

Richard Demarco Gallery 1966-76: 1975

Gladstone's Close
... Edinburgh

Richard Demarco 99

Edinburgh Arts Europe '76 was an unbroken 'journey' which covered 7500 miles in 70 days – it began on Tuesday, June 8, 1976 in Malta. Many exhibitions resulted from the experience of the 'Journey'. There were 'actions' by two artists from The Los Angeles Women's Building, Anne Gauldin and Barbara Bouska. Their powerful ritualistic performances questioned deeply the attitudes of an essentially male dominated art world.

The gallery concentrated on an extensive theatre programme called 'Atelier '76' during the Festival itself, proving its value as an arts centre. The programme ranged from a film on the Whirling Dervishes by Diane Cilento to an anthology of Brecht's songs by Eliza Ward of the Royal Shakespeare Company, and a production of *Antigone* by the Royal Scottish Academy of Music and Drama.

The crowning event of the Festival was Tadeusz Kantor's Cricot 2 production of *The Dead Class* at the Edinburgh College of Art. It proved to be a tour de force and created much controversy among Festival-goers and among the London art and theatre world cognoscenti when it was transferred to the Riverside Studios, Hammersmith after a short stay at the Sherman Theatre, Cardiff.

With this the gallery showed once again its responsibility to support artists even when they question, to the breaking point, the boundaries which separate art galleries from theatres.

In contrast, the post-Festival exhibition of paintings and designs for theatre by octogenarian, Jean Hugo, presented at the gallery and in association with the French Institute at their Randolph Crescent Gallery space was a quiet reassuring experience of a vision of the world of tranquility.

This was planned to run concurrently with an exhibition of the visionary image Margot Sandeman has made with acrylic paints on paper around her Arran island studio, evoking everyone's brighter memories of Hebridean sunsets in a landscape decorated by the timeless movements and forms of flocks of sheep. This anniversary exhibition will close on the same day the Edinburgh Arts Europe 76 Exhibition will open. This merging of the one into the other is perhaps symbolic of the Gallery's past being fused into its future linked with the experimental space provided in the age old concept of a journey made in the spirit of a pilgrimage, investigating the distant parts where lie almost obscured the vital origins of European culture.

Thus the gallery in considering its future looks to the past to gain the necessary forward momentum at a difficult but exciting time. The symbol of the Edinburgh Arts Europe 77 project and this life-giving movement is the prehistoric image of the spiral – which is to be found both in the Maltese temples and their Hebridean and Orcadian equivalents.

Richard Demarco Gallery 1966-76: 1976

KIBBLE PALACE · BOTANIC GARDEN GLASGOW   richard demarco 79

Why is Edinburgh not at least as well known as Paris? Why has Edinburgh not produced her Utrillo, her Pizarro, her Monet, her Buffet ? Is Edinburgh any less dramatically inspiring than Paris?

I choose to paint Edinburgh because I want everyone to share my joy in her. I want her citizens to see how extraordinary their ordinary everyday surroundings are.

I want the visitor to miss nothing, to see more than the obvious, more than the Castle and Princes Street. I want them to see the humour in the shape of Edinburgh chimney-pots and roofs and crow-stepped gables, the drama of plunging townscapes glimpsed through the mouth of a close.

There is an essential joy about living in Edinburgh that no other city can provide for me: not San Francisco or Rio, despite their superb balance of man-made beauty and nature; not Paris, for Paris is too large; not brand-new Brazilia, because it is brand-new: not even Florence or Munich or Copenhagen, because ultimately I am committed to the British way of life. It is the joy of her sudden-ness, her accessibility, her profound beauty that one can rediscover over and over again, on foot, from medieval huddle through Georgian elegance to wild sweeping hills, all within the one city boundary. And from my front door in Frederick Street I can walk within minutes to two great art galleries, to theatres, to concert halls, to spacious gardens and to the best of the city's shops.

In her composition, Edinburgh is a compound of miracles, an enchantment which no town-planner in his senses would ever have dared to dream: King's park, a displacement of the Highlands within 20 minutes' walk from the G.P.O. (can Hyde Park or the Bois de Boulogne compare?): a constant blending and re-blending of townscape and hillscape and seascape, the eye constantly drawn upwards to theatrical crags and battlements or downwards through medieval silhouettes: strings of sudden villages – Duddingston beside its loch in the lee of a high hill, Cramond hugging the banks of its river, Dean snug in a deep valley by the Water of Leith only a few hundred yards from the West End, Swanston with its thatches hidden on the Pent-land slopes.

From New Saltire review, August 1962

ADVOCATES' CLOSE

Richardbewar 1989

There is no such thing as an ordinary street scene. At each moment something extraordinary and even fantastic is happening which can be too easily taken for granted. The artist who finds it necessary to comment on the visual world cannot afford to miss anything worth recording in that street even if it is simply the momentary play of sunlight upon an ordinary brick wall which suddenly reveals a rich textural pattern and an infinite variety of reds and browns hitherto hidden.

The artist must look for the humour and drama produced by the juxtaposition of two unlikely objects as when, for example, a lamp-post appears to grow out of the roof of a passing bus. He notices how scaffolding can transform a nondescript building into an architectural fantasy. He sees the ever-changing rhythms of movement in a crowd of pedestrians and the balance of colour and shape in the clothes of people in a bus queue. He is aware of the transformation which takes place in the appearance of a housewife encumbered with parcels: the human being and the objects she carries have merged their identities to make something altogether different.

The artist is conscious of scale and space and the fact that sometimes it is necessary to ignore space in order to emphasise the dramatic relationship of things contrasting in scale. This enables the artist to see how a tiny distant figure appears to be walking on the gigantic shoulder of a person near at hand. The artist's curiosity is aroused by the half-observed lettering on a time-worn poster and this could infuse mystery into a commonplace background. His sense of the dramatic is stimulated by the sight of washing dancing gaily in a drying wind or of children skipping in a game of hopscotch.

The artist cannot pass a sight which could even be considered as ugly, for in a half-demolished building his attention will be held by the strong pattern and design inherent in wallpapered walls and fireplaces brutally laid bare to the public gaze.

Graceless street furniture also will have a value: imagine how the unutterable redness of a telephone kiosk can heighten the dramatic intensity of any street scene, or how a police box designed like a miniature Greek temple can introduce a note of incongruity and humour.

From: Why I Painted Edinburgh, Douglas & Fowlis catalogue, August 1962

Lock Gates. Union Canal Basin   Richard Demarco 1963
EDinburgh.

RAILWAY stations have always intrigued me. I derived inspiration from them as an art student, and I was pleased eventually to acquire a reputation as a painter of Edinburgh's suburban stations. Now I am inspired by them as a gallery director. I see Edinburgh's Waverley almost as an art form in itself.

Under its glass roof even the most ordinary subjects become transformed and reveal themselves as forms of painting and sculpture. A form of total theatre takes place every day in 'The Waverley'.

The crowds of London bound travellers move around 'The Flying Scotsman' as if organized by an inspired film director. There is no need for specially composed music to heighten the sense of drama, for there is that glorious cacophony of sound which only a station can make. This is nearer to the experience I sometimes find in the best avant-garde theatres or galleries.

In this way any of London's 19th century terminal stations are in competition with The Round House or The Institute of Contemporary Arts, and of course they have the advantage of being better known to the general public. It is perhaps unfortunate that in many new terminal stations including Euston, the dramatic experience of the platforms and the trains is not immediately felt.

A terminal station is a form of crossroads and, in fact, a market place. The arts can thrive there. It is where the traditions of our theatre were born with the medieval strolling players and their miracle plays. We really don't know if we need any form of art until we have experienced it.

If the art galleries of Britain were as much used as railway stations, I should feel much less worried about the problem of our young painters and sculptors graduating from our art colleges into a society which cannot employ them except in the capacity of schoolteachers.

I like the Tate on Sunday afternoons when the very atmosphere resembles a crowded railway station. The innumerable gallery goers are almost more compelling than the art they came to view. I dislike deserted art galleries or theatres as much as I dislike deserted stations.

This exhibition, 'Glass and Reflective Surfaces for Architecture,' will be seen by a vast multitude who will be discovering the work of contemporary visual artists for the first time. All the 25 participating artists will be pleased to see their work exhibited in a building which in itself is proof positive that we have need of their talents as artists, prepared to use the latest methods and materials incorporating glass and reflective surfaces.

With this exhibition, British Rail's London Midland Region has become an art patron on the grand scale. This is as it should be, for it is the responsibility of the State to excel in art patronage. The exhibition might indeed be of historic importance. It could be heralding 'A New Railway Age' in which British Rail's splendid new terminal stations could have a role to play as significant to the development of our cultural life as any national or state supported theatre or art gallery.

Foreword for Euston exhibition, October 1973

STORM Bound

Marketing The Visual Arts, Challenge and Response is the title of a handsome and expensive-looking book published by the Scottish Arts Council. The printers and designers have to be congratulated. They have surely given Professor Leslie Rodger good reason to be pleased, for his views on marketing have been packaged in such a way that no marketing expert could fail to be impressed. Whether it will impress the majority of artists in Scotland remains questionable.

Professor Rodger teaches at Heriot-Watt University. His qualifications to teach marketing techniques and philosophies are impeccable. The Scottish Arts Council are to be congratulated for giving him the commission to write the book which in their view would help their client organisations, responsible for the manifestation of the visual arts in Scotland, to cope with the Brave New World now planned by British Government policy, in which visual artists as well as performing artists and writers can expect to find satisfactory levels of patronage emanating almost exclusively from the market-place.

As the Scottish Arts Council seems to endorse this policy the book has the function of an instruction manual, laying out the basic rules of survival techniques for artists in order to survive in a materialistic age of rampant consumerism. The book in this way acknowledges the fact that, unlike the classical age of Greece or Renaissance in Italy, artists nowadays cannot expect to seek patronage around the 'Sanctum Sanctorum' provided by the physical presence of the cathedral defining a complementary and compensatory space to the market. This is a space in which art is used as visual evidence of that most unmarketable of human activities, the act of prayer, which once made saleable becomes automatically sacrilegious.

The book should certainly be useful to all those artists who have persuaded themselves that their art is marketable and who wish to collaborate with art gallery directors and dealers who agree with them. These are the artists who could probably cater for that vast majority of the general public who regard art as an up-market aspect of good decoration and design, who believe that art, for the most part, exists as a form of entertainment and as a way of dealing with the ever increasing time available for what are called 'Leisure Activities'.

Leslie Rodger has too intelligent and enquiring a mind not to know that there exists also a disturbing, well-nigh anarchistic force in society which is always asking the most awkward questions and telling unpalatable truths which even the most honest, well-intentioned politicians are incapable of acknowledging. The artist who is prepared to ask such questions will also be the one who knows that art at its most sublime is a form of prayer, a hymn of praise to the dialogue which God in heaven dares to have with all human creatures, and not only the living, but with the dead and all those yet unborn representing every aspect of the 'Communion of Saints'.

Rodger must know that there are gallery directors who know full well that "art is no laughing matter" and that if it encapsulates a really important moral, political, economic or social truth, that truth will be in existence for an insupportably long period of gestation before market forces can begin to operate.

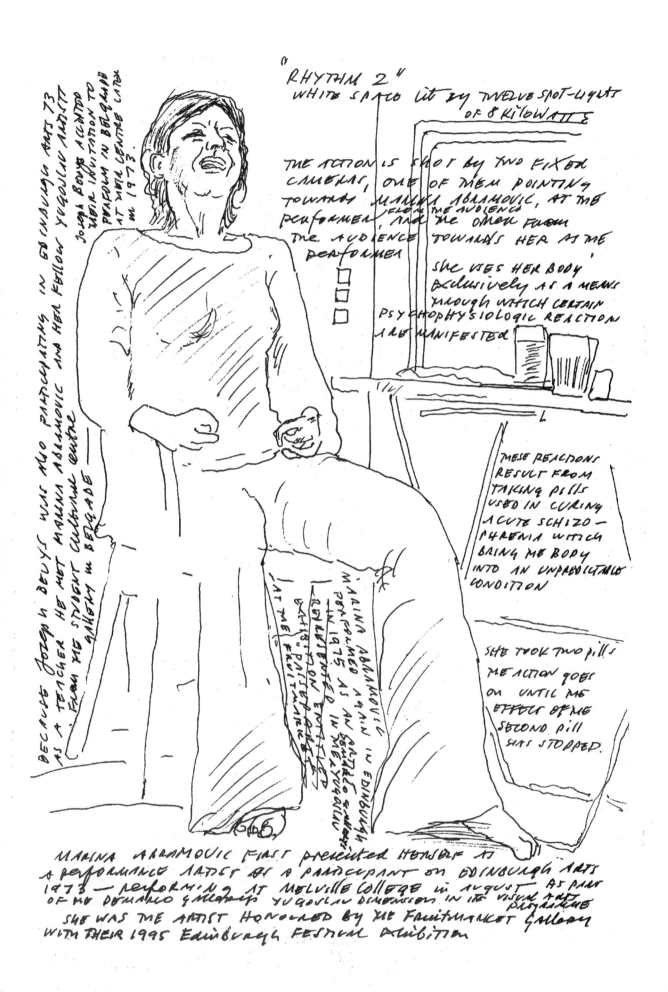

"RHYTHM 2"
WHITE SPACE lit by TWELVE SPOT-LIGHTS
OF 8 KILOWATTS

THE ACTION IS SHOT BY TWO FIXED
CAMERAS, ONE OF THEM POINTING
TOWARDS MARINA ABRAMOVIC, AT THE
PERFORMER FROM THE AUDIENCE, AND THE OTHER FROM
THE AUDIENCE TOWARDS HER AS THE
PERFORMER

SHE USES HER BODY
EXCLUSIVELY AS A MEANS
THROUGH WHICH CERTAIN
PSYCHOPHYSIOLOGIC REACTION
ARE MANIFESTED

THESE REACTIONS
RESULT FROM
TAKING PILLS
USED IN CURING
ACUTE SCHIZO-
PHRENIA WHICH
BRING THE BODY
INTO AN UNPREDICTABLE
CONDITION

SHE TOOK TWO PILLS
THE ACTION GOES
ON UNTIL THE
EFFECT OF THE
SECOND PILL
HAS STOPPED.

JOSEPH BEUYS ACCEPTED
THEIR INVITATION TO
PERFORM IN BELGRADE
AT THEIR CENTRE LATER
IN 1973

BECAUSE JOSEPH BEUYS WAS ALSO PARTICIPATING IN EDINBURGH ARTS 73
AS A TEACHER HE MET MARINA ABRAMOVIC AND HER FELLOW YUGOSLAV ARTIST
FROM THE STUDENT CULTURAL CENTRE ....
GALLERY IN BELGRADE —

MARINA ABRAMOVIC
PERFORMED AGAIN IN EDINBURGH
IN 1975 AS AN
REPRESENTED ENTITLED
ARTIST ON BEHALF OF THE
AT THE FRUITMARKET
BALKANO GALLERY
IN EX-YUGOSLAVIA

MARINA ABRAMOVIC FIRST PRESENTED HERSELF AS
A PERFORMANCE ARTIST AS A PARTICIPANT ON EDINBURGH ARTS
1973 — PERFORMING AT MELVILLE COLLEGE IN AUGUST AS PART
OF THE RICHARD DEMARCO GALLERYS YUGOSLAV DIMENSIONS IN ITS VISUAL ARTS PROGRAMME
SHE WAS THE ARTIST HONOURED BY THE FRUITMARKET GALLERY
WITH THEIR 1995 EDINBURGH FESTIVAL EXHIBITION

Van Gogh in his own lifetime personifies this kind of revolutionary artist whose art sprang not only from his essentially religious vision of the physical world, but also from his capacity to feel compassion for his fellow men. A whole century had to pass before that art which he made changed from being a totally unmarketable product to the most desirable product imaginable.

We must not be more amazed by someone's desire to possess a painting by Van Gogh entitled 'Irises' for a price of over fifty million dollars than by Van Gogh's own desire to paint the painting in the first place, and by Theo his brother's desire to help keep Vincent working as a painter against all the odds and all rational processes of thought.

The fact must surely have been considered by the Scottish Arts Council in giving Leslie Rodger his brief that art for Van Gogh as a genius was not about dealing with needs. It is on the contrary about desire, especially about desiring something which the world appears not to need within the framework of the market-place.

Picasso had to hide his 'Demoiselles d'Avignon' even from the art world of 1907, because although it was a true acknowledgement of the real space and time around his studio he knew better than any dealer that the *fin de siècle* spirit still held sway. Perhaps Stravinsky, who in the same year first presented his *Rite of Spring* to the sound of jeering from an abusive audience, would have been one of the few representatives of the human race alive at that time who would have had the courage to look at the terrifying 'Citoyennes' of Avignon and know they were a visual equivalent of his music; and therefore valuable beyond price.

It was significant that of all the representatives of the Scottish art world whom Leslie Rodger interviewed only William Jackson, as Director of the Scottish Gallery and Art in Business, earns a salary totally related to the number of objects he sells every year without expecting any support whatsoever from the Scottish Arts Council.

Every other representative of the Scottish art institutions upon which Leslie Rodger focused his attention is dependent for his/her survival upon not only Central Government funding through the Scottish Arts Council, but also funding from local authority sources.

The Scottish Arts Council knows full well the weaknesses at the heart of the Scottish art world. First, there are not enough commercial galleries and no sign yet of a commercial gallery area even in Edinburgh or Glasgow, a Scottish equivalent to London's international art market as defined by the Cork Street and Bond Street galleries and auction houses.

Even more saddening, there is not the slightest sign of developing areas of private patronage, representing the energies of individuals or institutions with their eyes upon the contemporary and international art world. There is no Saatchi Collection, no Gulbenkian or Henry Moore Foundations, no Contemporary Arts Society. Even the much publicised new School of Glasgow painters are still dependent upon patronage as far afield as New York and London.

THE FLIGHT TO BERLIN

Whilst on the flight, I handed George Wyllie a copy of a book entitled "OF MONKS & MARINERS" by ROBIN ARNOTT. I had bought it last week because it was about that part of the FIRTH OF FORTH which attracts me as an expression of all the voyages over the centuries which have marked Edinburgh as a capital city linked by sea to all the capitals of Europe.

There was a photograph of INCHCOLM ISLAND on the cover, the island made famous by its association with ST. COLUMBA that great priestly traveller, whose travels linked Scotland and Ireland. I had used the island twice, in 1988 & 89 to present "MACBETH" Shakespeare's master work. Shakespeare writes of it as "ST. COLM'S INCH" ("INCH" being the old Scottish term for "ISLAND")

George Wyllie found inspiration from the book. Yes! It was offering him the ideal solution to the problem of finding a suitable Edinburgh Festival location for his sculpture tentatively entitled "32 SPIRES", a work using trees from each of the 32 counties in both Ireland & Ulster. The island of St. Columba (the EAST COAST version of IONA) could provide the well-nigh perfect location for a sculpture celebrating the unifying aspects of the Celtic tradition. Beyond the Forth lies the Baltic — and the historic sea routes to Poland, Germany, the Baltic states and Russia and all of Scandinavia as well as the Mediterranean via the Channel, the Belgian, Dutch, French, Iberian coast towards Italy & the Aegean.

THE LAND OF MACBETH'S WITCHES WHICH BROUGHT BOY'S FRAU TO SCOTLAND

THE KINGDOM OF FIFE AT KINGHORN WHERE MACBETH WON HIS BATTLE WITH THE VIKING (NORWEGIAN) — KING SVENO.

Inchcolm Abbey.

A note of total unreality is struck when Leslie Rodger advises gallery directors to consider employing marketing experts, and I am thinking of Edinburgh's Collective Gallery and Glasgow's Transmission Gallery, which both survive on ludicrously inadequate budgets and are to a large extent dependent on the family of impecunious artists who have created them as places of serious experiment. Such institutions are by their very nature possessed of few patrons capable of arguing their case with captains of industry.

So who will make use of this book? Not William Jackson, who is a seasoned veteran of the international arts market; not museum directors whose main concern is fine art as a form of education and whose main interest is in art history and scholarship. It is not for those artists still young and idealistic enough to be naturally subversive, or those among their friends and patrons who support them in their acts of artistic endeavour. It could be written,

although I prefer to think it cannot be so, for a new breed of arts administrators who are specially educated and authenticated by the Scottish Arts Council itself, modelled upon all those graduates in arts administration from London's City University and who see a career in the visual arts as something honourable and acceptable. as a part of a valuable growth industry and secure enough to merit that kind of salary and pension such as executives enjoy as employees of Scotland's business and banking institutions.

In his introduction to the book Leslie Rodger asked the reader to think of it as a route map which sets out to answer such questions as "Where are we heading?", "Where do we want to go?", "What things should we look out for to help us reach our destinations?", "Who might we look for to help us on our way?"

Those questions strike a note of personal concern and respect for those who labour in the world of art.

I trust the Scottish Arts Council officials who helped bring Leslie Rodger to feel he had an emotional commitment to help artists with his advice will help him see that the answers should be contained within a much needed second book, a sequel to the first.

This could give the answers put directly to the following categories of people who seem to have been disregarded in *Marketing the Visual Arts*. They are, of course, first, the artists, the makers of art, without whom there would he no visual art world for the Scottish Arts Council to consider; and second, there would be the patrons of art, those who already buy as private individuals or as representatives of institutions: those, in fact, who represent the present state of visual arts patronage in Scotland.

Thirdly, there are those who teach and study art, those who represent the wellsprings of visual art activity in Scotland, and they should not be restricted to representatives of the four Scottish art schools. They should include all the art teachers and pupils in terms of local authority and private education. Good art education even at primary school level should prepare everyone in society to play the role either of artist or art patron.

After all, Joseph Beuys, the most influential artist imaginable representing the spirit of this day and age, spoke as both an artist and an art teacher when he said "Everyone is an Artist."

If Joseph Beuys was right to say that, then all four questions asked by Leslie Rodger will require him to consider a book of much more than a mere 72 pages in order to cope with the enormity of the 'challenge' and what could be a mind-boggling response, because, I feel that Beuys as an artist would have agreed with Strindberg's words: "Art exists to rid us of our demons", knowing as he did that western European society is bedevilled by the heresy inherent in late 20th century materialism.

Extracted from an article first published in Cencrastus 29, *Spring 1988*

PAUL NEAGU'S "ACTION" AT THE ROUND TOWER
Glendalough — EDINBURGH ARTS 1976

In 1974 the preliminary approach to the world of Meikle Seggie was made around the sacred hill of King Arthur and his Court – King Arthur's Seat, 'The Magic Mountain.'

In 1975 as the Demarco Gallery had moved to the old medieval city of Edinburgh, the journey actually began at the Gallery's front door, at that part of the Old Town known as The Royal Mile, and that part of the Mile where the High Street joins what is called Canongate, at that precise section where the City Gate stood marking "The World's End", separating the City and its Royal Palace on the Castle Hill from the place of sanctuary of the Canons of the Abbey of Holyrood built around the Royal Palace of the Holy Rude, or the Holy Cross.

The Meikle Seggie Road will only be found by those prepared to make proper use of all the signs and symbols which lie outside the front door of the gallery, and particular attention should be paid to the existence of an ancient well, almost the first significant thing to be seen outside the gallery's entrance.

It is a relic of the 17th Century water system which pumped water all the way from the Pentland Hills over a distance of five miles right into the medieval heart of the City, from what were called the Comiston Springs, named the hare, the owl, the rod and the lapwing, into five wells on the Royal Mile. Thus the gallery's front door can be marked by one of these, known as the Fountain Well.

My drawings are in homage to the mystery of that well in its present form, and to the energy it represents.

A few yards farther down the slope of the Royal Mile is situated John Knox's house, a notable piece of Edinburgh's medieval architecture with a good piece of advice inscribed into its wall for all travellers towards Meikle Seggie – "Love God Above All and Your Neighbour as Yourself".

From The Road to Meikle Seggie 1978

THE ROAD TO MEIKLE SEGGIE
AT SCOTLANDWELL

Richard Demarco
1976

The Royal Park of Holyrood is best explored following the three sacred lochs which help give the impression that indeed it is a Scottish Highland landscape, somehow displaced, and dramatically and unexpectedly set in the very centre of the city.

The first loch you see is called St. Margaret's Loch. Above its dark waters on a precipitous outcrop of volcanic rock stand the ruins of the Chapel of the Knights of St. John of Malta, and a reminder to all Edinburgh Arts participants that the road to Meikle Seggie must encompass the great Maltese Megalithic lunar observatory of Hagar Qim, and Mjnadjra. Beside the Chapel an enormous boulder marked the site of St. Anthony's Well. What is the connection between St. Anthony of Padua, patron saint of lost objects and the Crusaders?

Following the upper road which encircles Arthur's Hill you find St. Margaret's Loch, at a height of 500 feet above the Firth of Forth. There you could imagine on a dark moonlit night the sight of Excalibur, held above the deep waters which provide a dramatic foreground to the upper reaches of the Magic Mountain as they form themselves into the shape of a recumbent lion.

Arthur's Seat is thus revealed to take the shape of the legendary Royal Lion of Scotland, but sometimes at sunset it looks more like an Egyptian Sphinx.

Following the lines of the prehistoric terracing you climb to the summit. From this high and sacred vantage point all of the Lothians landscapes are revealed as the "Land of Lyonease", down to the South West to the Lammermuir and Moorfoot Hills, and to the Pentland Hills which begin within the City's boundaries, half as high again as Arthur's Seat 822 feet summit.

From: The Road to Meikle Seggie 1978

FLESHMARKET CLOSE

Half Way House

fleshmarket close, edinburgh   richard demarco
                                                    '89

To reach Meikle Seggie you must walk up the Radical Road back into the Canongate. Investigate all the Royal Mile closes and wynds, particularly Fleshmarket and Advocates' Closes, walk towards the battlements of Edinburgh Castle, to the Chapel of St. Margaret, then down the Castle Hill towards Edinburgh's other hills, particularly the Calton Hill, with its Observatory, and check out the routes which lead towards Craigmillar Castle, past Duddingston Village and its Romanesque church and Duddingston Loch, on the Western slopes of Arthur's Seat, which offers a perfect sanctuary to hosts of migrating birds.

Search out the most northerly point of the Great Pilgrimage Route to Compostella, the 15th Century chapel of the Earls of Roslyn. It is the last flowering of the Medieval stone masons' craft. Seek out beside the High Altar 'The Apprentice Pillar'. It has, unlike all the other pillars supporting the nave, the spiral energy of a tornado.

Explore the vast moorland spaces between the Moorfoot and Pentland Hills around Howgate Village; at Crichton Castle note the 16th Century Italianate courtyard built by the Earl of Bothwell. Then move towards the 12-mile long coastline of Edinburgh from Portobello and Leith towards Granton and Cramond, where the Romans sent their supply ships to build the Antonine Wall. Walk along the beaches strewn with white seashells which mark the north-eastern boundary of the Rosebery Estates and consider why Miss Jean Brodie spent the happiest hours of her prime on this coast which leads to South Queensferry.

Looking from the windows of the Hawes Inn, from which Robert Louis Stevenson was inspired to write Kidnapped, you will observe the gigantic cantilever forms of the old Forth Bridge, the greatest piece of monumental Victorian iron-work sculpture in Europe.

From: The Road to Meikle Seggie 1978

I recognise the road as far away as the Maltese Islands by place names such as Hagar Qim, Mdina, Rabat, Xlendí and Mgabba, and by some which are in Italy, at Alberobello, Martina-Franca, Atina, Verese and Picinisco, and in France at Carnac, Brignognan, Vence, Roscoff and in Yugoslavia at Motovun, Mostar, Zagreb and Sarajevo.

The Scottish, Welsh, Irish and English place names are virtually unknown to those who plan journeys with the help of tourist guide books.

These names sometimes define villages and towns such as Cerne Abbas, Echt, Tarbert, Zennor, or mountains, hills and hillocks at Knocknarea, Robin Hood's Stride, Kes Tor and Goat Fell, or prehistoric temples, burial mounds and dolmans at Sun Honey, Cairnpapple, Castle Rigg, Pentre Ifan, Bryn Calli Ddu, Knowth, Giurdignano, Barumini, Nuoro and Scor Hill; or churches and chapels at Rosslyn, Abbotsbury, Brechin and Torphichen, and gardens at Edzell, Brodick, Chatsworth and Haddon, Eagle's Nest and T'a Torri, or sacred pools and wells at Youlgreava, Les Trois Fontaines, La Fontaine du Peyrat Vance, Fontaine aux Colombes Vence and La Fontaine da Puyrabier, Gencay.

Alleyways, lanes, closes, wynds, and all small scale, man-made townscape spaces are part of it in the form of Borthwick's Close, Castle Wynd in Edinburgh, and Triq Sent Orsla in Sanglea, Rio Santa Fosca in Venice and Cardinal's Alley in London.

All come easily to my mind as I write and I long to allow myself the pleasure of penetrating their winding, ever-mysterious confines.

From: The Road to Meikle Seggie 1978

GHARB CHURCH, GOZO WITH
SAINT'S DAY DECORATIONS.   Richard Demarco '69

The Edinburgh Arts 1978 Journey is 7,500 miles in length. It will of necessity incorporate the Road to Meikle Seggie. It will begin and end at the sacred hill of Arthur's Seat and at The Demarco Gallery.

It will extend as far south as the Island of Malta and the prehistoric temples of Hagar Qim, the Maltese equivalent of the Orcadian Ring of Brodgar.

It will have taken into account our modern world, and the signs, symbols and artefacts representing past layers of time; the Renaissance, the Middle Ages, the Classical World of Rome and Greece, and the world beyond time – the world in which dwell King Arthur, Gawain, the Green Knight, Merlin, Ulysses, Calypso, St. Serf and Queen Maev; that time and space which all artists know well when they use the full force of the poetic imagination, the immeasurable temple of our day-dreams and the longings of the human heart.

My instinct tells me to make drawings and paintings of the Road to Meikle Seggie, not just along its ten-mile length, but when it manifests itself through the tales of the Arthurian Knights and the Argonauts, and the present-day adventurers they personify the painters and sculptors, who work with the inspiration of Lugh.

I can draw or paint the tangible and observable markers, tracks and trails they leave behind them when they travel in harmony with The Goddess, so my drawings and paintings are about what I see in the real world all round me.
They are about the magic in all things we recognise as normal.

They are not about the paranormal.

From: The Road to Meikle Seggie 1978

WHO IS THIS MAN
AND WHERE IS
HE WALKING
TOWARDS WITH
SUCH CLEAR PURPOSE
WITH HIS CROOK AND
HIS BELL??

EDINBURGH ARTS
IS MEANT TO HAVE
SOMETHING TO THINK
ABOUT ON THE
ROAD TO IONA

KILLADEAS CHURCHYARD. FERMANAGH - SIDE VIEW   R. DEMARCO

The Road to Meikle Seggie exists for me as a physical reality, but it works more importantly as a metaphor for all the roads which lie beyond it in our imagination. It also represents that land or space I should dearly like to see honoured and protected and extended in our own times, that particularly beautiful man-made landscape or townscape whether it be Tuscany, Somerset, Puglia, Cumbria, Sardinia, Brittany, Argyll, Pembrokeshire, Venice, Salisbury, St. Paul de Vence or the Trossachs.

All are beyond the plans of any one generation of architects. All are about generations of farmers, fishermen and craftsmen, knowing instinctively how to use local materials to best advantage. Not one was built as an environment for tourists.

It seems that architects and town planners are no longer allowed to build such places. Our over-rational building regulations will not allow for the degree of irrationality required for any decant building to ba built with the builders taking full responsibility for every stone as it is placed upon another.

Only when we learn again to honour the Goddess will the lessons of the Road to Meikle Seggie be taken into full account in all our future buildings of environments, and in the way we will probably make the things we need for our journey through life. Only when we know how to take full responsibility for, and to love, all man-made things will we make them pleasing in our own eyes. They accompany us on our journey through life. They must not confuse or hinder us.

They must be so constructed that we could pass them on, no matter how well worn, to those who must follow our trails, to those who could use them possibly as markers or maps or instruments, tools and even talismans.

This rule applies to all things we make, even the most humble chair, or table, wheelbarrow, cart or walking-stick, and the most basic gear and tackle – even our working clothes and all our writings, drawings and paintings. Then there are the corner windows and doors of our resting places, and in particular that special place where we feel most 'at home'.

This special place is, of course, our own special abode, our very own nest, where we feel most closely in touch with the complexity of our all times past, not only in our own lives, but also in the lives of our forbears, and more importantly with Mother Earth. This special place must be seen to be what indeed it is – our home, but also the most far distant destination of all our journeys.

From: The Road to Meikle Seggie 1978

Richard Demarco
1963

THE SAILORS' Church AT HONFLEUR

If you follow St. Serf's footsteps on the motorway northward from the Firth of Forth you could find yourself in the centre of Milnathort. There on the old main road north through the town centre you will observe an official Kinross-shire county road sign indicating that Meikle Seggie lies nor-nor-west whilst Stirling lies to the north-west and Perth to the north-east. Over the next two miles you will find it difficult to discover the next signpost for Meikle Seggie. Be content to follow the sign to the Path of Condie. Eventually you will find, by then following a sign to the Ochil Hills Hospital, that the Meikle Seggie signpost is a small, inconspicuous, hand-made wooden sign, pointing towards an ordinary single track road at a right angle to the Milnathort-Ledlanet road, two-miles from Ledlanet House, John Calder's Scottish version of Glyndebourne.

Before you reach this point you could be beguiled and misled by other signs indicating – Tillywhally, Glenfarg, Dunning and Nether Tillyrie.

You will find Meikle Seggie with perseverance and the instincts of a traveller in a fairy tale who keeps a lookout for signs and symbols in trees and bushes and the general lie of the land itself, and who knows that every step depends upon a flying detail – a falling leaf, a ray of sunlight, the flutter of a bird's wings.

Your faith in the significance of Meikle Seggie could be tested when you discover, after travelling for only 200 yards, that Meikle Seggie could be what appears to be a farm-steading with its name, handpainted, on a sign almost overgrown in an ordinary garden hedge. Take heed, the road continues unsignposted alongside the hedge, beckoning you upwards into the hills.

Do not be misled by handpainted signs to Seggiebank, Pathstruie, West Hall, Craigow, for now you are truly on the road to Meikle Seggie, to the sites of unnamed ancient uninhabited farmhouses, often in a state of ruin.

They will help give you the feeling that you have penetrated into Scotland's past. Here, you will find the road begins to climb gradually over wild rolling moorland. Then unexpectedly the road begins to curve downhill towards the widest imaginable panorama of hills, lakes and mountains, from Fife to Perthshire and even into Coupar Angus.

From: The Road to Meikle Seggie 1978

JUST OVER ONE MILE FROM THE OFFICIAL SIGNPOST IN THE
HIGH STREET OF MILNATHORT YOU COULD COME
ACROSS THIS LESS IMPRESSIVE SIGNPOST (NOT AN
A.A. AUTOMOBILE ASSOCIATION STANDARD) JUXTAPOSED
WITH THE SIGN TO LEDLANET HOUSE IN THE
'SEVENTIES' STILL THE HOME OF JOHN CALDER.

LEDLANET 1¼ MILES

MEIKLE SEGGIE

WESTHALL

SEGGIEBANK

CRAIGOW

IS MEIKLE SEGGIE JUST A FARM OR
A LOST SETTLEMENT?

IS THERE A MOMENT WHEN YOU CAN RESIST A MOZART OPERA AT LEDLANET
AND THE LIFE ENHANCING WORLD CREATED BY JOHN CALDER IN THE OCHIL HILLS
AND TURN TOWARDS MEIKLE SEGGIE?

I have called this road 'The Road to Meikle Seggie' because actually it does not lead to a town, village or hamlet, but only to a farmyard called 'Meikle Seggie' which marks the site of an ancient settlement now considered too unimportant by map-makers, and beyond that inconspicuous farmyard it leads to everything in Scotland that I know and love.

It is a road at one with nature, it follows the lie of the land – rising, falling, turning, twisting, like a living thing. It does not detract in any way from the untouched landscape of rolling hills. It led today to the villages of Newton of Pitcairns and Dunning. It could have led to Forgandenny or Glenfarg, depending on which direction you take at two T-junctions after you have travelled five miles.

Dunning defines the *Sunset Song* Scotland of Lewis Grassic Gibbon with its small-scale, single-storey weavers' houses, brightly painted and much loved in the best possible tradition of Scottish domestic architecture, and its magnificent Romanesque church with its saddle-back steeple.

There is a road leading from the Tron Square to the Yetts of Muckhart. I must go there; it is a possible extension of the road to Meikle Seggie. But today I was content to retrace the journey from Dunning to Pathstruie to enjoy again the breathtaking panoramic view which is revealed by the road just as it begins to descent from its highest point on top of the Ochils, two miles from the Path of Condie.

The Ochils form the southern wall of the great Perthshire valley which stretches from Perth to Stirling. You can see this thirty-mile long stretch almost in its entirety as well as the wall of the Grampian mountains which form its northern boundary, stretching in the west from the slopes of Ben Lomond to the mountains beyond Glenalmond to the Killour Forest.

From: The Road to Meikle Seggie 1978

TRAVELLING ON ME ROAD TO MEIKLE SEGGIE IT IS ADVISABLE TO READ G.K. CHESTERTON'S VIEW ON THE IMPORTANCE OF FAIRY TALES IN HIS ESSAY — "THE ETHICS OF ELFLAND"

LET US TAKE ONE PRATICAL EXAMPLE OF ME TRUTH OF FAIRY TALES. IN THESE STORIES SUCCESS IS MADE TO DEPEND ON A NUMBER OF SMALL MATERIAL OBJECTS AND OBSERVANCIES; LIFE IS A CHAIN OF TALISMANS. IF A MAN TOUCHES THREE TREES IN PASSING HE IS SAFE; IF HE TOUCHES FOUR, HE IS RUINED. IF ME HERO MEETS A MILLER HE IS TO ANSWER NONE OF HIS QUESTIONS. IF HE PLUCKS A RED FLOWER IN A PARTICULAR MEADOW, HE WILL HAVE POWER OVER ME MIGHTY KINGS OF SOME DISTANT CITY. NOW THIS POETIC SENSE OF ME DECISIVNESS OF SOME FLYING DETAIL IS A THOUSAND TIMES MORE GENUINE AND PRACTICAL THAN ME POMPOUS INSISTENCE ON SOME MORAL OR SCIENTIFIC LAW

GLENFARG 6
MILNATHORT 6½

IS THIS THEREFORE A MAGIC SIGNPOST? ?

NONE OF US KNOW WHEN WE HAVE DONE SOMETHING IRREVOCABLE. OUR FATE HAS OFTEN BEEN DECIDED BY THE TWIST OF THE ROAD OR ME SHAPE OF A TREE — AND THERE CAN THEREFORE BE LITTLE REASON FOR DENYING THAT IT IS A MAGIC ROAD OR A MAGIC TREE "

10-15 AM - 3 MAY '73
— RICHARD DEMARCO

AT ME PASS OF CONDIE (ALSO CALLED PATHSTRUIE) WHERE THE MAY WATER FLOWS UNDER A 300-YEAR OLD STONE BRIDGE, BESIDE TWO OLD CROFTS, THERE IS AN OLD METAL ROAD SIGN WITH ONE OF ITS ARMS BADLY BROKEN SO THAT IN MAKING THE DECISION TO TURN LEFT YOU CONTINUE IN THE SPIRIT OF ADVENTURE AND WITH FULL RESPECT FOR ME MYSTERY OF ME ROAD TO MEIKLE SEGGIE YOU HAVE TO FORSAKE ME KNOWN FOR ME UNKNOWN, FOR ME REASSURING FACT THAT MILNATHORT IS 6½ MILES DISTANT FOR ME UNCERTAINTY THAT 5 MILES DISTANT IS A DESTINATION DEFINED BY ME LETTER "Y"

Just outside Dunning to the right of the road beyond the rolling fields, I could see a castle far off on the side of a hill. There was an old ruddy-faced man walking on the road wearing a deerstalker hat and a long black coat. I felt that possibly he could lead me to the Scotland of the 1920s and to my favourite heroine in Scottish literature, the very personification of Scotland's earth spirit – Grassic Gibbon's Chris Guthrie. Within minutes I was to sea the land of the North East through Chris Guthrie's eyes. What was revealed was her world.

As the road climbed steeply to over four hundred feet I saw, by the light of the sunset dominating the North West horizon, the jagged outlines of the high Grampian peaks, beyond the rolling plains of the rich Strathearn farmland which were decorated by patches of woodland, long hedgerows and stone walls.

The cloud-filled sky and the hills and mountains shared the same colour scheme: cold purples and blues contrasted with warm greens and yellows and blacks and whites where the snow had fallen on ploughed fields, and in the dark mountain valleys and in the cowering masses of clouds.

The road to Meikle Seggie had proved itself to be a dramatic event indeed, my favourite form of theatre. There are few 20th century refinements about it, and virtually no traffic. There are at this vantage point, where the road curves around a farm at a place called Middle Third, no signposts or road signs, so you know the age of the motor car has almost forgotten its existence – it remains an ancient track through the hills; a cattle drovers' road, an 18th century highway which grew naturally from the landscape it traversed.

The Road to Meikle Seggie should not be limited to this age. It does not fulfil the usual requirements of a 20th century road. It is not for the 1978 traveller or modern concepts of progress. I wish to draw, with pencil and pen, its form, the line it already makes in the landscape – a living line made by man, not boastful or pretentious, but quietly confident with proper consideration for the most subtle movements of the rolling earth.

Even as I write it is changing as the hours creep forward to the full summer days.

From: The Road to Meikle Seggie 1978

Dunottar Castle

Richard Demarco

The Road to Meikle Seggie is the gateway to the Scotland which eludes most Sassenachs (and that surely includes most tourists). To find it from Edinburgh you must head northwards on the main motorway. It will take you through the valley between the Cleish and Lomond Hills where you will first glimpse the Ochil Hills as the introduction to wild, unspoiled, unchanging mountainous land, where the elemental forces are forever in control.

Take the road to Meikle Seggie and you have made a true beginning to your journey through Scotland. It lies twenty miles from Edinburgh's boundary at Barnton.

It exists for ten precious miles as itself, but in that sheer distance it teaches you many things so that you will search for the forms it acquires when it takes other names and finds extensions of itself – the single track roads to Newton of Pitcairns and Forgandenny and to the Yetts O'Muckhart through the Glen Devon Forest, and the road to Wicks O'Baiglie, which must inevitably lead into The Kingdom of Fife to Augask and Newton of Balcanquhal.

It will lead you to the distant Grampians, to the Broom of Dalreoch or Muthill with its Romanesque church reminiscent of Dunning Church, and past rows of 19th century weavers' cottages and past the gardens of Drummond Castle to the hill town of Crieff.

From there you can journey either westwards to St. Fillans on the shores of Loch Earn, or directly northwards through Gilmerton and the wild splendours of the Sma' Glen to Amulree and Glen Cochill where the vast enchanted spaces of the Highlands will fill your mind and soul with the eternal truths they represent. You will pass Loch Na Craige before descending steeply to Aberfeldy and its fertile valley and will surely be led on to the land of Appin of Dull due westwards to that splendid example of a complete Gothic-revival village of Kenmore.

From: The Road to Meikle Seggie 1978

prehistoric
burial chamber
— ONE OF FIVE
in the Kilmartin
valley

St. Martin of Tours
and St. Columba in the
valley of "Kil-
Martin"
"Saint-Martin"

Pollalloch

pollalloch

Pol
CA
alloch

BURIAL EFFIGIES OF
THE LORDS OF THE ISLES
Richard Demarco '92

IN KILMARTIN
GRAVEYARD

My concern for the 'Road to Meikle Seggie' is beyond reason. It was not discovered by a rational, ordered sequence of events. I first sought it out when I decided not to attend a Mozart opera at the Ledlanet Festival, and felt I needed to rethink my apparent need of an art experience. I discovered it as an alternative to art.

I wanted a road to nowhere, one I could not find on any map where I could, on a certain evening, see the western sky in the late evening light. I knew it was the road westwards, although it begins in an easterly direction.

I knew it would confuse the seeker of that kind of information which leads inevitably to a place where twentieth century man has been before. The very confusion of the signposts, even their existence at crucial points where vital decisions have to be taken, cause me to ignore them and to rely on the instinct which obliges me to make landscape drawings.

When I am asked why I see Edinburgh Arts not as a time and space emphasising the making of art, but rather as a time for reflection, rediscovery and opportunity to make art statements which relate directly to Scotland, and its cultural heritage stretching far back into history – not trusting an explanation, I tell the story of my discovery of the road to Meikle Seggie.

It is the metaphor which explains my need to draw and paint Scottish landscape and, at the same time, continue the adventure of Edinburgh Arts.

From: The Road to Meikle Seggie 1978

Temple Wood, Kilmartin Valley — The Heartland of
The Kingdom of Dalriada — The Scots — Richard Demarco

I have managed to re-discover the long-lost 'Road to the Isles'; I call it the Road to Meikle Seggie. It crosses that fateful frontier that separated the world of the Celt from that of the Roman, and therefore the English-speaking Lowland Scot. Properly negotiated, this road to Meikle Seggie leads into a part of Scotland that would surely challenge and alter any Italian artist's concept of Europe, particularly when the road crosses over that point where the waters – of the Burn of Sorrow intermingle with those of the Burn of Care, falling through seven waterfalls in the valley of douleur (Dollar Glen) beneath the stern walls of Castle Campbell.

Meikle Seggie does not exist on any normal map of Scotland, but I can assure my Italian friends it does exist if you take seriously the legend of St Serf and the Dragon of Dunning.

One of the most important exhibitions in the first year of the Demarco Gallery's existence was the presentation of 37 artists representing the Italian post-war avant-garde – a collaboration with the Galleria Internationale d'Arte Moderna in Rome. It was the experience of this exhibition, which afterwards went to the Ulster Museum in Belfast and the Museum of Modern Art in Oxford, that led me to develop relations between Scotland, East European countries such as Poland, Romania and Yugoslavia and what I regard as their Western equivalents: France, West Germany and Italy.

I was happy that I had dealt first with Italy, because it was the first European country in modern times to test Scotland's capacity to welcome foreigners into a social structure that had been. for most of the 19th century, cut off from foreign influences.

Being an Italo-Scot meant that I had been born into the largest and most significant group of foreigners, who for no logical reason had sought to retrace the steps of the Roman legionaries, all the way from the Appenines and the Alps to the Ochils and the Grampians, at the turn of the century when Italians had their first opportunity to explore the world beyond the Mediterranean. So I was to grow from childhood to adulthood expecting Italo-Scots to spread throughout their new homeland and inhabit even the most remote extremities of Scotland – as far north as Kirkwall, as far south as Stranraer, as far east as St Andrews. as far west as Stornoway.

From: My Scotland, 1988

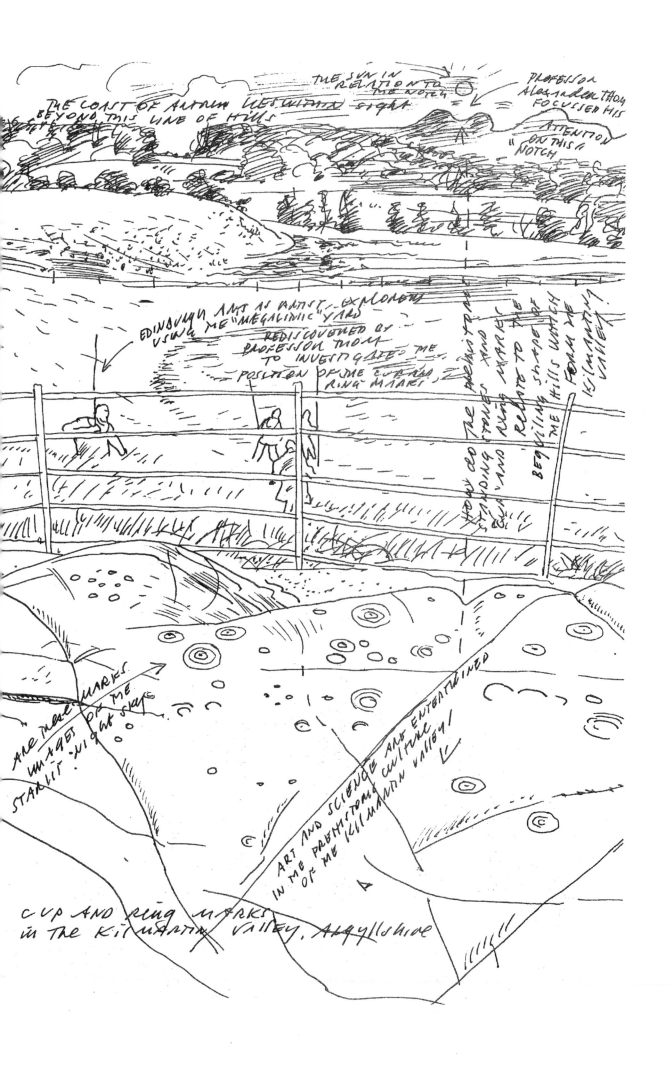

THE COAST OF ANTRIM LIES WITHIN SIGHT BEYOND THIS LINE OF HILLS

THE SUN IN RELATION TO THE NOTCH

PROFESSOR Alexander Thom FOCUSSED HIS ATTENTION ON THIS "NOTCH"

EDINBURGH ARTS AS ARTIST-EXPLORERS USING THE "MEGALITHIC" YARD

REDISCOVERED BY PROFESSOR THOM TO INVESTIGATE THE POSITION OF THE CUP AND RING MARKS

HOW DO THE PREHISTORIC STANDING STONES AND CUP AND RING MARKS RELATE TO THE BEGUILING SHAPE OF THE HILLS WHICH FORM THE KILMARTIN VALLEY?

ARE THESE MARKS UN TAGET OF THE STARLIT NIGHT SKY?

ART AND SCIENCE ARE ENTERTWINED IN THE PREHISTORIC CULTURE IN OF THE KILLMARTIN VALLEY

CUP AND RING MARKS IN THE KILMARTIN VALLEY, ARGYLLSHIRE

TODAY IS My Birthday. That is the title Tadeusz Kantor gave his last work as an artist. He died in the act of creating it. Surely this is the way he would have wished to make his farewell gesture to the world of twentieth century art.

It was made in the only space where his agonised soul found satisfaction on this earth. This was where he rehearsed and conducted his fellow artists as actors. It was where he chose to fight his wars against what he used to call 'the pseudo avant-gardistes', 'the ciquettes' (his word for a social gadfly), 'the tamed', 'the mass-producing'.

He knew he was out-numbered and his little band of guerrilla fighters were on all sides liable to be overwhelmed.

His advice to them was straightforward. "A demarcation line must be made everywhere and always quickly and firmly, as it will function anyway whatever we choose to do, automatically and relentlessly, leaving us at this side or the other." The line would place him among "the few, the unofficial, the neglected, the risktaking, those not afraid to be ridiculous.

Kantor's actors were prepared to follow him all over the world. They were known and honoured as 'The Cricot II Theatre'. In time, Kantor referred to them as 'The Impossible Theatre' and 'The Theatre of Death'. Their origins were to be found in the theatre world of Krakow in the Thirties.

He was in rehearsal in his beloved city of Krakow last Friday, when he died of a heart attack. His mind was concentrated upon January 23, the date when the Parisian art world would be provided with further evidence of his genius. He had won the respect of French theatre-goers, long before he was recently awarded the Légion d'honneur by President Mitterand.

He had, from his earliest student days, been deeply impressed and inspired by Stanislaw Ignacy Witkiewicz, the painter-playwright and exponent of the Polish avant-garde between the two world wars. *Today is My Birthday* will never be performed even by the Cricot Theatre for the simple reason there was never a possibility of even one Cricot performance occurring without Kantor's physical presence. He was like a great composer, conducting his own music with his own symphony orchestra. He had little respect for anyone in theatre who would be content to direct a play without taking full responsibility for what is normally in the hands of set and costume designers, and lighting experts, even musicians.

ZBIGNIEW GOSTOMSKI AS LEADER OF THE 40 MANDELBAUMS A CROWD OF RELIGIOUS FANATICS

THE CLOAKROOM MACHINE

SOPHIA KALINSKA AS THE PRINCESS KOENIGSBRAGA ESCAPING FROM THE CAGE.

SANDY NAIRNE AS A TEMPORARY MEMBER OF THE CRICOT THEATRE PLAYING THE ROLE OF THE MAN (IN THE CLOTHES OF A BISHOP) OPENING AND CLOSING A DOOR

EXIT

LET

WIESLAW BOROWSKI MISSIONAIRE IN SWANGEUCHOLA AT THE MULTI

MAN CAUGHT IN TRAP.

MALIA STANISLOT AT THE WASHBA WOMAN OPERATING A MANGLARD MACHINE

TADEUSZ KANTOR

SALLY HOLMAN AS LIAISON BETWEEN THE CRICOT THEATRE AND THE DEMARCO GALLERY

A BREAK IN THE CRICOT THEATRE'S REHEARSAL
OF 'LOVELIES AND DOWDIES' AT THE POORHOUSE
THIS WAS TADEUSZ KANTOR'S VIEW OF STANISLAW WITKIEWICZ'S
MASTERPIECE.   EDINBURGH ARTS STUDENTS AND ACTORS
AND ARTISTS WERE INVITED TO PARTICIPATE BY ATTENDING
REHEARSALS AND ATTEND WHAT WERE IN FACT TADEUSZ KANTOR'S
MASTER CLASSES.   AMONG THOSE WHO ATTENDED WERE JENNY
AGUTTER, TINA BROWN, AND JOSEPH BEUYS.

During the late fifties and sixties, Kantor staged several happenings pre-dating the infamous Allen Kaprow/Mark Boyle 'happening', at the 1963 Edinburgh Festival Writers' Conference, inspired by John Calder. After 1963 he began to define most of his paintings as *'emballages'*. The term referred not only to the technique of wrapping objects, but also to his attitude to the object as an extension of the human figure portrayed as a carrier of packages, forever in transit. The figure became an object. seeking the lowest rank in the order of man-made things.

It was Wieslaw Borowski, as Director of Warsaw's Foksal Gallery, who first introduced me to Kantor. In 1969 he was the good friend of Rsyzard Stanislawski, the Director of the Museum Sztuki in Lodz, who had suggested I should seek Kantor on his own home ground in Krakow. where there existed the Krzysztofory Galler, like the Foksal, a place where serious artists congregated, and Kantor's ideal underground theatre. In June 1972 I followed the Cricot II to a small theatre in the Malakoff suburb of Paris to see Kantor work with a company of French and Polish performers in a production of Witkiewicz's *Les Cordonniers.*

One month later the Demarco Gallery introduced the Cricot for the first time to the English-speaking theatre world at the Edinburgh Festival. They presented, at my request, not *Les Cordonniers* but *The Water Hen,* arguably Witkiewicz's masterwork. I offered a theatre space which would provide as near as possible the conditions of Krakow's wartime underground theatre world.

The space was a semi-derelict plumber's workshop on the site of the medieval Edinburgh bedlam. This was the 'Poor House,' whose walls defined the perimeter of the histone Greyfriars Churchyard.

On his third visit to the Festival in 1980, Kantor was pleased to accept his long-awaited 'Fringe First' for his production of *The Dead Class.* By. then, the 'Poor House' had been long condemned as unsafe and unsuitable as a Festival Fringe venue.

The Dead Class was performed in the Edinburgh College of Art Sculpture Court – a fitting location for what was essentially a work of kinetic sculpture and a spectacularly successful art lesson.

Kantor was honoured by a major exhibition at the Whitechapel Gallery, and in New York at the La Mama Theatre he won a coveted 'Obei' Prize, which he was to win again for his production of *Let the Artist Die.* This was inspired by the wanderings and humiliations of Wit Stoss, the early Renaissance master of wood sculpture.

Kantor identified himself with Wit Stoss, whose altar-piece in Krakow Cathedral provided an early source of inspiration. Kantor recognised himself in the trials and tribulations suffered by Stoss.

The achievement of Tadeusz Kantor is that through his own unique artistic expression he brought into focus not only Witkiewicz, but an entire generation of Polish artists, writers and composers, who must now surely find their rightful place in the mainstream of the newly unified cultural identity of Europe.

R. DEMARCO 72

DIRECTED, DESIGNED AND
CONDUCTED BY TADEUSZ KANTOR

"THE WATER HEN" BY STANISLAW WITKIEWICZ
A CRICOT TWO THEATRE PRODUCTION IN THE GALERIA KRZYSZTOFORY, CRACOW

Kantor himself was an inspired actor and teacher. All his actors knew he could perform their roles better than they dared imagine. Joseph Beuys and Tadeusz Kantor should have been naturally wary of eaeh other. After all, Poland had suffered much from those who, like Beuys, fought for the Third Reich. I introduced them to each other in the relaxed setting of my Edinburgh living room during the 1973 Edinburgh Festival.

I knew then they were deeply respectful of each other. Indeed, as a result of their meeting, Beuys happily performed under Kantor's direction for one performance of *Lovelies and Dowdies,* another Witkiewiez classic. In this he created a 'domain of the impossible'.

The heroine was the Princess Abenceraga, played by Sofia Kalinska. as a beautiful temptress, a lioness, a revolutionary and a match for all her enemies, including members of the audience who were trained during the performance to act as a crowd of 'Forty Mandelbaums' (the pre-war Polish term for a Jewish religious extremist. As religious fanatics, they feared her beauty and mystery and capacity to see, with unerring instinct, the inadequacy of their misplaced masculine authority. The entire action took place in a cloakroom. The audience were corralled and numbered as had been citizens of wartime Krakow. Imagine that night when the audience contained Sean Connery, Auberon Waugh and Tina Brown.

Born in 1915 in Wielopole. a small village near Krakow and not that far from Auschwitz, Kantor graduated from the Art Academy of Krakow in 1939, the year of Witkiewicz's suicide. From 1940 to 1944, he presented his theatre literally underground, in cellars beneath the heels of the Wermacht. In this way he kept the gentus of Witkiewicz alive.

In these productions and in his creation of 'Cricot II', he developed the language of theatre in which the linear continuity of the written text was broken down within a stage action which became simultaneous and multifocal, with all the characters talking at once, or two actors playing the same character at the same time.

WHEN I EVENTUALLY MET Joseph Beuys IN THE WINTER OF 1970, HE WAS FULLY
OCCUPIED WITH HALF-A-DOZEN FRIENDS WHO OCCUPIED HIS SMALL STUDIO
WHICH SERVED AS A RECEPTION AREA AND OFFICE, AN EXTENSION OF THE
UNOBTRUSIVE HOUSE IN WHICH HE LIVED IN THE OBERKASSEL DISTRICT OF DUSSELDORF
WITH HIS WIFE EWA. AND TWO YOUNG CHILDREN JESSYKA AND WENZEL.   I WONDERED
WHAT I COULD OFFER THAT WOULD MAKE HIM CONCENTRATE HIS ATTENTION UPON
SCOTLAND, THE VERY PERIPHERY OF THE INTERNATIONAL ART CONTEMPORARY ART
WORLD. I DECIDED NOT TO ASK HIM TO MAKE A NEW AND SPECIAL ART
WORK AT THIS TIME, BUT TO CONCENTRATE INSTEAD UPON THE SIMPLE, OBVIOUS AND
UNIQUE NATURE OF SCOTLAND'S PHYSICAL BEAUTY DEFINING THE SEA-GIRT WESTERN
EXTREMITY OF EUROPE.
OVER TEN MINUTES I SHOWED HIM A COLLECTION OF POSTCARDS OF SCOTLAND.
HE EXAMINED EACH AND EVERY CARD. THEIR SUBJECT MATTER WAS A MIXTURE
OF HEATHER AND HEATH; MOUNTAIN STREAM AND WATERFALL; FORESTS & FIELDS;
deer AND SHEEP AND HIGHLAND CATTLE; THE MIDSUMMER SUNSET OVER ISLANDS;
CELTIC AND PICTISH STANDING STONES. AFTER A LONG SILENCE HE REMARKED:
"I SEE THE LAND OF MACBETH; SO WHEN SHALL WE TWO MEET AGAIN IN THUNDER
LIGHTNING OR IN RAIN, WHEN THE HURLEY BURLY'S DONE, WHEN THE BATTLES FOUGHT
AND WON.
   FOUR MONTHS LATER JOSEPH BEUYS ARRIVED IN EDINBURGH, ACCOMPANIED BY
KARL RUHRBERG AND GEORGE JAPPE.
   I DECIDED TO TAKE JOSEPH BEUYS ON THE ROAD TO THE ISLES' INTO THE
CELTIC WORLD OF THE MOOR OF RANNOCH.

JOSEPH BEUYS ON
RANNOCH MOOR

RICHARD DEMARCO
MAY — 1970

I had learned, through Cranley School's contribution that 'small is indeed beautiful' and that art could be wedded successfully to education without the use of 20th century gadgetry. I found myself a witness to a form of total theatre. They presented me with the self same experience I had known when I had become a part of the 'animated paintings' of Joseph Beuys and Tadeusz Kantor.

Cranley used the word 'tableau' but what I witnessed was beyond a 'tableau vivant'. Like Beuys and Kantor's expressions of art, they dispensed with any normal concept of a stage area separating performers from audience.

I discovered that I and every other member of the jury were being invited to play a role in the action which told us much about our own lives as citizens of Edinburgh. The real Polish waiters had served real Polish vodka to their Forresthill audience; the Cranley girls served real Edinburgh scones and cakes and tea to the jury.

As with the action of *Celtic Kinloch Rannoch* and *The Water Hen,* the Cranley presentation not only activated the mystery of present time but reactivated by and recalled the mystery of the past. The action incorporated all those aspects of visual artso theatre and music which I had first discovered integrated in the philosophy of theatre created by the Cricot artists.

Cranley had managed to make a living out of its own reality, of its staff and students as a community intimately related to the very fabric of their school building. The limitations of space and facilities were made into a positive advantage.

Unlike all the other schools which tended to disguise their building's interior to make an art experience which referred to other spaces, Cranley used the very doors and windows, both the exterior and and interior spaces of their physical world. They emphasised the very 'Edinburgh-ness' of their building, by focusing upon the sense of history in the architectural details.

IN JANUARY & FEBRUARY I BEGAN MY EXHIBITION PROGRAMME FOR THE
EIGHTIES' WITH AN EXHIBITION HONOURING THE ACHIEVEMENT OF
CRANLEY SCHOOL IN WINNING THE FIRST PRIZE IN THE LIFE ASSOCIATION
OF SCOTLAND'S 1978 COMPETITION FOR LOTHIAN SCHOOLS — INVITING
TEN SCHOOLS TO CONSIDER THE THEME OF "EDINBURGH IN THE THIRTIES"

I WAS ON THE JURY WHICH JUDGED THE COMPETITION. WE VISITED TEN SCHOOLS.
I ENJOYED THE PRESENTATIONS OF TWO LOCAL AUTHORITY SCHOOLS, BROUGHTON AND FORRESTER.
THE BOTH PRESENTED DIVERTING AND PROFESSIONALLY STAGED MUSICAL ENTERTAINMENTS
WHICH MADE SPLENDID USE OF THIRTIES MUSIC AND DANCE TRADITIONS.
GEORGE WATSONS MADE AN EXHAUSTIVELY DETAILED STUDY OF RELIGION
IN EDINBURGH WITH PARTICULARLY INTERESTING INFORMATION ON PARISH
LIFE IN EDINBURGH'S PRESBYTERIAN CHURCHES. LINLITHGOW ACADEMY
TRANSFORMED THE INTERIOR OF AN OUTBUILDING TO RECREATE
THE INTERIOR OF A SUBURBAN HOUSE
OF THE THIRTIES
IN EDINBURGH

CRANLEY SCHOOL'S CONTRIBUTION QUITE OVERWHELMED MY SPIRIT ALLOWING
ME TO EXPERIENCE A "TOTAL ART WORK" — BRINGING TOGETHER ALL ASPECTS
OF THE VISUAL AND PERFORMING ARTS.

JIM SOUNESS, THE GENERAL MANAGER OF THE LIFE ASSOCIATION OF SCOTLAND
WROTE THE FORWARD TO THE EXHIBITION AS FOLLOWS — "THE REAL REWARD FROM
SPONSORING THE SCHOOLS' COMPETITIONS IN 1978 AND 1979 WAS TO EXPERIENCE THE
DIFFERING DEPTHS OF ARTISTIC INVOLVEMENT CREATED BY THE COMPETITORS. AT ONE LEVEL
ONE WAS LOOKING AT A VISUAL PRESENTATION, AT THE NEXT LEVEL ONE WAS WATCHING A PERFORMANCE
BUT THE WINNING LEVEL IN 1978 ONE WAS SURROUNDED BY THE ENTRY. MY PERSONAL OPINION
IS THAT THE CRANLEY CREATION WAS THE OUTSTANDING ENTRY OF THE TWO YEARS".

The 'performance' began before you entered the building. You made a ritual entry through the 'threshold' of the main door into the reception hall. There you were confronted with an almost full-scale Edinburgh tramcar moving towards you, for as you entered what at first looked like a tableau of a 1930's street scene, all the countless figures in the street suddenly came to life, including the tram.

The sound of the tramcar bell immediately evoked memories of my daily journey to school on the number twelve tram from Portobello to Leith. For a moment I thought the jury was in danger of being knocked down by a terrifyingly real tram.

This was a true 'coup de théâtre'. The tramcar was so positioned that it added a three dimensional reality to a mural which revealed in striking details the 1930's life of Princes Street. This mural prepared your eyes for the variety in the groups of figures going about their daily lives. There were children playing street games, street urchins, tramps, out-of-work miners, housewives cleaning their front-door steps and stairways.

There were shoppers buying their food from totally authentic displays in greengrocers, fish-mongers, bakers. All these groups revealed aspects of working class life in the Depression years. The conversations that could be overheard were all about the everyday lives I remembered of my uncles and aunts and their friends. In direct contrast to this you were then gently but firmly led into an interior space of a large salon-like room.

In this, every imaginable aspect of middle and upper class Edinburgh life was there to be observed at close quarters a trio of very respectable musicians struck up that kind of 'Thé Dansant' café music which I had heard as a 19-year-old child on my first visits to the restaurants of Jenners and Patrick Thomsons department stores. The jury were invited to sit down and enjoy afternoon tea. Snatches of fascinating chit chat could be heard.

Every imaginable Edinburgh character was there: gossiping, fur-coated Morningside ladies; gay young things chattin about their boyfirends and holiday plans; schools swopping their cigarette card collections, dressed in authentic gym tunics and straw hats.. They were obviously the kind of girls that Miss Jean Brodie in her prime would have regarded as 'la crème de la crème.'

A pompously efficient, moustachioed 'floor-walker,' possibly a veteran of the Scots Guards, helped oversee the splendid fashion parade which caused the conversations to move towards the cost of the latest fashions.

THE TOP FLOOR OF BLACKFRIARS STREET CHURCH
PROVIDED AN INSPIRATIONAL SPACE FOR ARTISTS
SUCH AS JOHN DAVID MOONEY MIMMO ROTELLA
PAULA REGO EMILY ASH TO MAKE THEIR ART
AS WELL AS WELL AS KRISTOF AND YAN LUZYNSKI TO MAKE
THE POLISH-RUSSIAN THEATRE PRODUCTION OF A STOP IN THE DESERT
AND FOR EWA WYCLCHOWSKA TO PRESENT THE "POLSKI TEATR TANCA BALET
FROM POZNAN IN FULLSCALE EXCITING DANCE PRODUCTIONS OF THE LONELINESS
AND JAMES O'BRIENS GIRO THEATRE PRODUCTION OF THE FAWN" AND KARMA.
OF REDEMANCE.

I SHOULD LIKE TO SEE CHESTER
THE SPIRIT OF THEIR TROUBLED
ALSO MUCH OF THE POLISH THEATRE
AND MEGA PRODUCTION OF A

AS WELL AS OAKHAM SCHOOLS GLORIOUS PRODUCTION
OR NBTO THE MUSICAL "COMPLETE WITH ORCHESTRA IN 1981.
AND RADLEY COLLEGE
REPERTORY HEREABOUTS COLLEGE PERFORM
THE CUCKOOS NEST WITH A PRODUCTION
STOP IN THE DESERT
LUBLIN - GLORIA CHWILOWA

I WON'T FORGET THE WINDOWS AND THE SOARING
WOODEN ARCHES - A PERFECT PLACE
FOR THEATRE.

OF COURSE IT WAS HERE THAT YVETTE BOSZIK
FIRST PERFORMED THE EDINBURGH FESTIVAL

THE GUARDIAN
JOYCE MACMILLAN WRITING IN 1989
I OUT OF THE DEATH THROES OF THE OLD SOVIET
EMPIRE COMES GAURA CHWILOWA'S INTIMATE
STOP IN THE DESERT
VIVID FOOTNOTE TO KANTOR'S
MEDITATION ON THE LIFE OF AN
ARTIST IN BRUTAL AND
DEADENING POLITICAL TIMES"

PRODUCTION OF TATTOO THEATRE
DISCOVERING MLADEN MATERIC
IN THE OBALA THEATRE IN SARAJEVO ON THE WINTER OF 1992
I KNEW I HAD FOUND A SPLENDID SPIRIT OF KANTOR'S CRICOT THEATRE

TATTOO
THEATRE

"TATTOO IS
COMPLETELY
ORIGINAL
MAGNIFICENTLY
PERFORMED
AND SUFFUSED
WITH A DEEP
BUT UNSENTIMENTAL
AFFECTION."
— THE TIMES —

WHEN I THINK OF BLACKFRIARS
STREET AS THE HOME OF
THE DEMARCO GALLERY

I THINK OF
MLADEN MATERIC
AND HIS PRODUCTION
OF TATTOO
THEATRE
MAKING
MANIFEST
THE CREATIVE
SPIRIT OF
SARAJEVO AT
THE 1997
FESTIVAL

The Eighties! A decade to remember. Eventful. Impossible. Challenging. Beginning with hopes of adventure on the high seas by means of the Edinburgh Arts 1980 circumnavigation of the British Isles on the sailing ship **Marqués.** The Demarco Gallery should have ceased to exist on a number of occasions when the adventures on land and sea involved impossible risk taking in order to keep up with the speed of change brought about by, above all, Joseph Beuys.

He was then, arguably, the most significant artist in all the art world, prepared to challenge the very nature of that world which he dominated as inadequate in the face of the overwhelming challenge of a new millennium.

The Demarco Gallery was ill-prepared to deal with the impact of Joseph Beuys' firmly held conviction that 'everyone is an artist' – including the inmates and staff of the Special Unit, H.M. Prison, Barlinnie. This meant a Joseph Beuys/Jimmy Boyle dialogue at the very moment when Jimmy Boyle was being obliged most reluctantly to return to the normal regime of strict incarceration at H.M. Prison, Saughton. There was a Joseph Beuys protest involving legal action against the office of the Scottish Secretary of State supported by Joseph Beuys going on hunger strike. A gallery which would bring about such events together with the idea of a two-month voyage linking Britain's centres of cultural and spiritual art activity was hardly in a position to reassure the Scottish Arts Council that art-making could be a well-behaved activity.

There were other artists who challenged the gallery to other breaking points. Royden Rabinowitch needed a dialogue with the European art world and the gallery gave him this through the support of such gallery Friends as Johannes Cladders, Rudi Fuchs, Declan McGonagle and Michael Bailey, who purchased one of his sculptures for the MacLaurin Gallery.

Royden Rabinowitch is a sculptor of outstanding intellect and commitment to the history of ideas through art, but he demanded the gallery's total involvement which was his due and which could only be properly served by of the European museums dedicated to avant garde art.

There was John Cousins, the New Zealand composer and performance artist, who made a work of art consisting of music made manifest by his bodily liquids being pumped by his sustained physical effort to fall dripping upon a sculpture of pipes and drums. Mind-boggling it was, indeed and the gallery was hard pressed to defend it against the attentions of the popular press.

This was part of the 1984 Anzart Exhibition at the Edinburgh College of Art. It introduced to Britain, or anywhere, for that matter, the first ever exhibition of both Australian and New Zealand artists.

SCULPTURE
IN
THE GARDEN
VILLA MOMMEN
MASSERIA
SPIGOLIZZI
PUGLIA

RICHARD DEMARCO
—1981—

1984 was the year of a twelve-day 'Demarcation' Conference on Art and the Human Environment which involved the New Zealand and Australian artists. It brought them and many other artists and art experts including Bruce McLean and Mark Francis together with environmentalists and those responsible for experimentation in other art forms such as Jonathan Miller and Sir Hugh Casson, Hugh Johnson and his brother Brian Johnson. Sean Fuchs and Fr. Kenneth Nugent.

This conference preceeded another in Dublin. It was entitled Art and the Human Environment – Dublin: A Case Study and was about a city collapsing under the impact of un-restrained materialism, but it brought together artists, ministers of culture and high-ranking politicians.

The Demarco Gallery worked under the inspired direction of Michael Murphy and his team who celebrated the glories of Dublin under the concept of 'Contemporaire' as a festival of the arts celebrating Dublin's longevity as a city.

Among the speakers were Lord Gowrie, Jack Lang, the Irish Taoisach, Gareth Fitzgerald, Charles Haughey, Gough Whitlam, Anthony Burgess, Rudi Fuchs, Pierre Restany, Johannes Cladders, Karl Ruhrberg, Jimmy Boyle, and that most intelligent of American collectors, the creator of the Dia Foundation, Mrs De Menil.

Prior to that, in 1983, as part of the Edinburgh Festival exhibition dedicated to the work of Count Giuseppe Panza Di Biumo, as an outstanding collector of avant garde art, the gallery presented a conference at Edinburgh University on the subject of Housing the Arts Towards the 21st Century. It was through this that the gallery introduced Count Panza into the world of another outstanding art patron, Dr. Arthur Sackler who as a New Yorker had thought fit to add a new wing to the Metropolitan Museum.

The gallery also had the responsibility of introducing Arthur Sackler to Michael Spens. the publisher of *Studio International,* so that this, the oldest visual art publication, would be given a new lease of life and be saved from severe financial problems.

In close collaboration with Arthur Sackler the gallery presented three exhibitions which represented nearly two million pounds worth of patronage for the Edinburgh Festivals of 1983, 1984 and 1985.

Vicolo con scale   VIESTE, GARGANO   Richard Demarco
                                                      1981

The gallery could not have begun the eighties on a more negative note because it did so having to vacate the premises it had rented from 1974 at Monteith House, on the Royal Mile.

Within a few months, that is from August 1980, the gallery was obliged to operate without adequate premises in a small office on the opposite side of the High Street at number 30. It was there that the gallery heard the news in November that the Scottish Arts Council had cut the gallery's annual grant completely and without due warning.

The gallery was obliged to depend on its Friends to support it. Chief among them was Joseph Beuys and as a result there came into being the now famous masterpiece Poorhouse Doors. This was Joseph Beuys' personal homage to the work of the gallery in what was known as The Poorhouse, an historic though thoroughly derelict building abutting on to the southern boundary of Grayfriars Churchyard at Forresthill.

When the gallery had raised nearly £40,000 from the support of 750 Friends the Scottish Arts Council restored their annual grant.

Although this represented a much reduced form of Central Government financial support it encouraged the gallery to operate out of a new rented space which had previously been a shop at 10 Jeffrey Street. This was thankfully nearby, just around the corner from the Royal Mile.

There the gallery remained for six years, from 1982 to 1987, when by the most generous decision of the Edinburgh City District Council the gallery was given the right to buy a splendid four-storey building in Blackfriars Street for the nominal sum of £10,000.

Through the most timely intervention, support and good advice of the architects, Nicholas and Limme Groves-Raines, the gallery began restoring and acquiring this building in 1988.

There were other artists who continued to test the gallery in this very building, particularly Paul Neagu and Mario Merz. This they did in 1988, in happy collaboration with Barbara Grigor and the Scottish Sculpture Trust which financed the two exhibitions, thus strengthening Scotland's cultural dialogues with Romania and Italy. **132/**

chiesa de L'Angelo Raffaele
Filippi The
ponte del Socorso   Richard DeMarco '81

venezia

With the Blackfriars Street building the Demarco Gallery was able to concentrate upon its theatre programme with the reassurance that at long last it had found a permanent space, contrasting to all the temporary spaces which the gallery had to rent from 1980 to 1967 – places such as Edinburgh's Franciscan Church hall, the Canongate Lodge Masonic Hall, St. Mary's Catholic Cathedral hall and various classrooms and halls in George Heriot's and St. Margaret's Schools.

However, in such rented spaces memorable productions took place, ranging from opera to satirical revue and to experimental theatre.

The gallery worked with some important personalities and companies to win more than its fair share of Edinburgh Festival Fringe awards and successes. There was the University of California at Los Angeles, Cambridge University Opera Society, the Free Shakespeare Company, Poland's Theatre of the 8th Day and the Dublin Theatre Company of Jim Sheridan, who was to achieve fame as the film director of *My Left Foot*. Many of the actors and directors involved have become household names such as Myriam Margoles, Charles Lewsen. Richard Crane, Faynia Williams, Neil Bartlett, Morwenna Banks and Tony Slattery who all gave their commitment to the gallery's concept of theatre.

The Blackfriars Street premises was to prove particularly inspirational to Mladen Materic's Obala Theatre Company from Sarejevo with their masterpiece *Tattoo Theatre* and the Italian theatre company La Zattera Di Babele directed by Carlo Quartucci and Carla Tato.

Their controversial production in Italian and English of Shakespeare's *Macbeth* enabled the gallery to use Inchcolm Island as a new venue for the Edinburgh Festival in collaboration with the Office of Scotland's National Historic Monuments. Their *Macbeth* began at the gallery and continued by road and sea to the Island of Inchcolm.

VIA MANZONI, RODI GARGANICO

Richard Demarco July 81

Throughout the eighties, whether with the benefit of suitable premises or not, the gallery developed its concept of education through journey, under the aegis of 'Edinburgh Arts.'

Twice the gallery directed its energies to Italy through 'Edinburgh Arts' journeys into the world of Count Panza di Biumo in Varese, Milan and Turin in 1982 and 1984; twice to the Venice Biennale in 1984 and 1988.

Other journeys were also made to the Netherlands, Belgium and Germany into the world of Johannes Cladders in Munchen Gladbach and Istvan Szenassy in Middelburg; as well as to Rudi Fuchs in the Van Abbemuseum, Eindhoven and the world of Dom Hans van der Laan and Dom Kees den Biesen in the Benedictine Abbey of St. Benedic-tusberg at Vaals near Aachen.

I have no doubt that Hans van der Laan has created the most beautiful twentieth century work of architecture with the new church and monastery of St. Benedictusberg. This is the answer to the heresy of all post-modernists. I wish with all my heart that Prince Charles could see this building of unutterable beauty, full of spiritual energy, both timeless and resolutely modern, an expression of everything that we could hope for in the architecture of today.

There were also four expeditions to Poland which enabled the gallery to introduce no fewer than 80 British, European and American artists and art patrons to Poland to extend dialogues with, for example, Tadeusz Kantor, Rsyzard Stanislawski, Wieslaw Borowski and Andrzy Kondicki.

Among the British artists who performed in Poland as a result were Alistair Maclennan, Anne Seagrave, Dymytro Morykit and Claire Thacker.

In Britain 'Edinburgh Arts' journeys were made in collaboration with George Wyllie to Rannoch Moor to celebrate the life of Joseph Beuys and his Scottish Symphony inspired by Rannoch Moor, entitled 'Celtic Kinloch Rannoch,' as well as journeys to the Marlborough Festival where the gallery presented, in collaboration with the Marlborough Festival organisers, spear-headed by Nick Fogg, two exhibitions of sculpture in 1988 and 1989 entitled the Windows of Marlborough.

This involved Mel Gooding, Neleke Fuchs, Elizabeth Chatwin and Peter Levi as jury members awarding prizes to those artists who had managed to make the shop windows of Marlborough High Street into works of art.

A PAPATODERO, LOCORONTONDO, PUGLIA   Richard DeMarco '81

Arguably the most important exhibition involving 'Edinburgh Arts' was the one made possible in collaboration with the Scottish Sculpture Trust and Peacock Printmakers, Aberdeen.

This presented over 50 Scottish artists at the Collegium Artisticum in Sarajevo. In a journey in January, 1988 which involved over 30 participants and inspired Paul Neagu, Arthur Watson, Marilyn Smith, George Wyllie, Lorna Green and Moira Innes to make site-specific sculpture installations. The journey involved everyone in dialogues with the art communities of Ljubljana, Zagreb, Belgrade, as well, of course, as Sarajevo.

To offset the inadequacies of its exhibition spaces, the Demarco Gallery was pleased to use the Edinburgh City Arts Centre to present major exhibitions of important senior Scottish artists such as Fred Stiven and Alastair Park in 1983. Alastair Park, the only Scottish artist to involve himself in a meaningful artistic dialogue with Beuys in 1970, died tragically at the height of his considerable powers in 1984.

It was in the City Art Centre that the gallery presented major exhibitions from the collections of Arthur Sackler at the 1983 and 1984 Festivals. In seeking 'international' spaces in which to show its artists, the gallery became deeply involved in the burgeoning world of Art Fairs in Britain. 1983 saw the beginning of a commitment to the Bath Art Fair which has continued to this day, as well as to Interbuild's art fairs at Olympia and the Barbican and more recently at the Business Design Centre in Islington. In 1986 the gallery participated in the Los Angeles Art Fair, selling prints by Joseph Beuys.

In the eighties the gallery had depended totally on the loyalty and hard work of its Friends and supporters, particularly the Board of Directors, and especially those who chaired the board. There have been four in all.

First there was Victor MacDougall, who completed five years of valiant service in 1980. James Ferguson, who fearlessly succeeded him, was prepared to face the agony of life without the Arts Council annual grant.

The ever-faithful John Martin, one of the original founders of the gallery, took over from him in 1984. He in turn, handed over the chairmanship to James Walker in March 1988. He, like John Martin, was a founder of the gallery. He dedicated himself to setting the gallery firmly on a course which would allow it to take responsibility for Scottish artists to work on their own home ground within an international framework, with particular reference to Eastern Europe, Japan, South America and, of course, all the countries that the gallery concentrated upon in introducing whole national schools of avant garde art into Scotland for the first time: countries such as West Germany, Austria, France and Ireland.

TOWARDS MONTE SAN MICHELE, ALBEROBELLO. PUGLIA.   Richard DeMarco
— July 81

Alas, the eighties saw the deaths of three members of the Board of Directors of the gallery.

The highly gifted artist, art patron, poet and musician Rory McEwen; Duncan MacFarlane, the most talented architect and art patron, and most recently Dione Patullo who decided to support the gallery from her experience of the 'Demarcation' exhibition of 1984.

For almost six years she served most loyally and energetically with the full support of her extraordinary family: her son Nicholas, who, alas, died tragically, all too young, and her daughters Sam and Nicola.

It can be said that without Dione Patullo and her extraordinary patronage, particularly of Mladen Materic and the Obala Theatre, the gallery would simply not have survived the severe testing it was obliged to undergo in 1987, 1988 and 1989.

Dione Patullo was indeed a true patron of the arts and an inspiration to everyone who knew her.

Certainly, one of the great triumphs that the gallery can claim to be associated with was that of the Obala Theatre's *Moonplay,* presented at last year's Festival by Dione Patullo, in association with the gallery in the exquisite temporary theatre space of the Grassmarket Mission.

If anything sums up the Demarco Gallery's commitment to its work of presenting works of experimental art it was this production.

At the same time the gallery had the energy to present another memorable production of *Macbeth.* This came into being within the impossible space of only twelve days through the indomitable spirit of John Bett and the extraordinary company of Scottish actors and musicians that he gathered around him to present his adaptation of Shakespeare's masterpiece on Inchcolm.

This replaced La Zattera Di Babele's production which was sadly cancelled due to illness.

Another high point of 1989 was the Phaidon Dinner in the splendid setting of the Signet Library. There, Peter Palumbo, as one of Britain's outstanding patrons of the arts, and Chairman of the Arts Council of Great Britian, H.E. Boris Bianchieri, the Italian Ambassador, and Sandy Nairne, director of visual arts at the Arts Council of Great Britain, all spoke honouring the gallery's work.

Under the generous patronage of George Riches, Chairman of Phaidon Press, the renowned international arts publishers, over 200 guests were given the opportunity to celebrate the gallery's life and work and consider its future. Sally Dunsmore, as Phaidon's press officer, worked wonders to organise this memorable event.

BETWEEN COWGATE & CANONGATE   Richard Demarco '89

The year 1990 marks the 24th of the gallery's existence and the 20th anniversary of the gallery's 'Strategy-Get-Art' exhibition. The plans are to present an exhibition of German art for the 90s which will hopefully give it the same kind of energy that it received through the impact of the German art world upon Scotland.

The gallery ended 1989 by providing space for over 250 Scottish artists. They showed their work under the proud banner of the Society of Scottish Artists led by their president George Wyllie. This was an historic event because it was the first time in 98 years that the SSA found their home at the Royal Scottish Academy Gallery unavailable.

The New Year will begin with the gallery presenting Polish art in collaboration with Southampton's Hansard Gallery and with an 'Edinburgh Arts' expedition to Poland from January 3 to 12 as a preparation for an even more testing expedition to both Poland and Ruggin from May 1 to 16. January 31 will see the private view of 'Art 90,' the London Art Fair at the Business Design Centre, Islington. The gallery will be represented by twelve artists.

I look forward to meeting all the gallery's London-based friends there and would remind them and everyone who cares about how Scotland relates to the international art world that for the first time ever, thanks to the extraordinary work of the Scottish Sculpture Trust, there will be a Scottish presence at the 1990 Venice Biennale.

That is only fitting in the year when the international art world spotlight is firmly fixed upon Scotland, with Glasgow in the role of European City of Culture.

I wonder what Hugh MacDiarmid, that great Scottish internationalist, would have made of Glasgow in such a role. One of the heartening sights for me personally was to see many of Hugh MacDiarmid's friends attend the three-day conference at the 1988 Festival talking and lecturing passionately about his work. The conference was in relation to an exhibition inspired by MacDiarmid's life.

With the support of the Gulbenkian Foundation there was a whole section of the conference dedicated to a posthumous dialogue between Hugh MacDiarmid and Portugal's Fernando Pessoa, another great poet, like MacDiarmid still underestimated in Britain. The language of art, in celebrating life, triumphs over death and I'd like to think that Hugh MacDiarmid and Fernando Pessoa are now involved in that dialogue that they deserved to have to had on earth and that Valda Grieve, who sadly died earlier this year, will be, as was her wont, deeply involved in contributing her own poetic dimension.

BITS & PIECES

A COLLECTION OF WORK BY JOSEPH BEUYS FROM 1957-1985
ASSEMBLED BY HIM FOR CAROLINE TISDALL

TEXT AND PHOTOGRAPHS BY CAROLINE TISDALL

FAT

THE FRONT COVER OF THE EXHIBITION CATALOGUE OF THE 21ST ANNIVERSARY EXHIBITION OF THE DEMARCO GALLERY PRESENTED IN BLACKFRIARS STREET AT PART OF THE OFFICIAL EXHIBITION PROGRAMME OF THE 1987 EDINBURGH FESTIVAL — AS A HOMMAGE TO JOSEPH BEUYS

THE EXHIBITION A TIMELY PROVIDED A REMINDER OF JOSEPH BEUYS PARLO AAODNESS TO EXHIBIT HIS WORK AT PAUL NEAGU GENERATIVE ART GALLERY IN LONDON IN THE SPRING OF 1976

JOSEPH BEUYS MADE EIGHT VISITS TO SCOTLAND — ALL UNDER THE AEGIS OF THE DEMARCO GALLERY — IN MAY AND AUGUST 1970 IN AUGUST 1973 — FOR ME HELD LECTURE 17 ON ANACHARSIS CLOOTS IN MAY 1974 FOR THE 3 POTS ACTION IN AUGUST 74 FOR EDINBURGH ARTS IN 1976 JAN IN SUPPORT OF JIMMY BOYLE IN AUGUST 1980 — FOR 10 ANNIVERSARY OF STRATEGY — GET ARTS IN 1982 AUGUST TO MAKE THE POORHOUSE DOORS INTO AN ART WORK

BEUYS BUTTER POTS 1983 — TWO STAGS SKULLS FILLED WITH BUTTER BEUYS SUGGESTS THROUGH THIS DOUBLE-IMAGE THE MIRROR-IMAGE IMPLIED THE IMAGE OF MOVING TO DEATH — HE USED ME IN MANY OF HIS EARLY DRAWINGS IT'S APPEARANCE OFTEN SYMBOLISES TIMES OF DANGER

BEUYS CONSIDERING THE THREE POTS ACTION

PUBLISHED BY THE RICHARD DEMARCO GALLERY
IN ASSOCIATION WITH
RED LION HOUSE AND THE ARNOLFINI GALLERY BRISTOL

Art originates in the meetings of friends and in their shared hopes, aspirations and values.

I firmly believe this and what is more, I believe, art is the one language we can use more effective than any other, to link we who happen to be alive upon this beleaguered planet, hurtling through space and time towards a new millennium, with the countless generations who have gone before us and those yet unborn.

I camot wish a Good New Year in a more appropriate way than to quote the eight lines of Hugh MacDiarmid's poem 'The Bonnie Brookit Bairn' which reveals his deep love, not just for humanity. but for planet Earth:

Mars is braw in crammasy,
Venus in a green silk goun.
The auld mune shak's her gowden
*   feathers,*

Their starry talk's a wheen
*   o'blethers,*
Nane for thee a thochtio sparin',
Earth, thou bonnie broukit bairn!
– But greet, an' in your tears ye'll
*   droun,*
The haill clamjamfrie!

As a footnote I may add that one of my favourite Scottish artists. Margot Sandeman will be featured on Channel 4's breakfast programme 'Box Office' on Thursday, January 4.

Television viewers will see her studio and the painting she made on the theme of 'morning'. I was privileged to be asked to be interviewed on her work.

It is inspired as so many of her paintings are, by her love and understanding of the shoreline of the Island of Arran, overlooking the Firth of Clyde and the far distant coastline of Ayrshire.

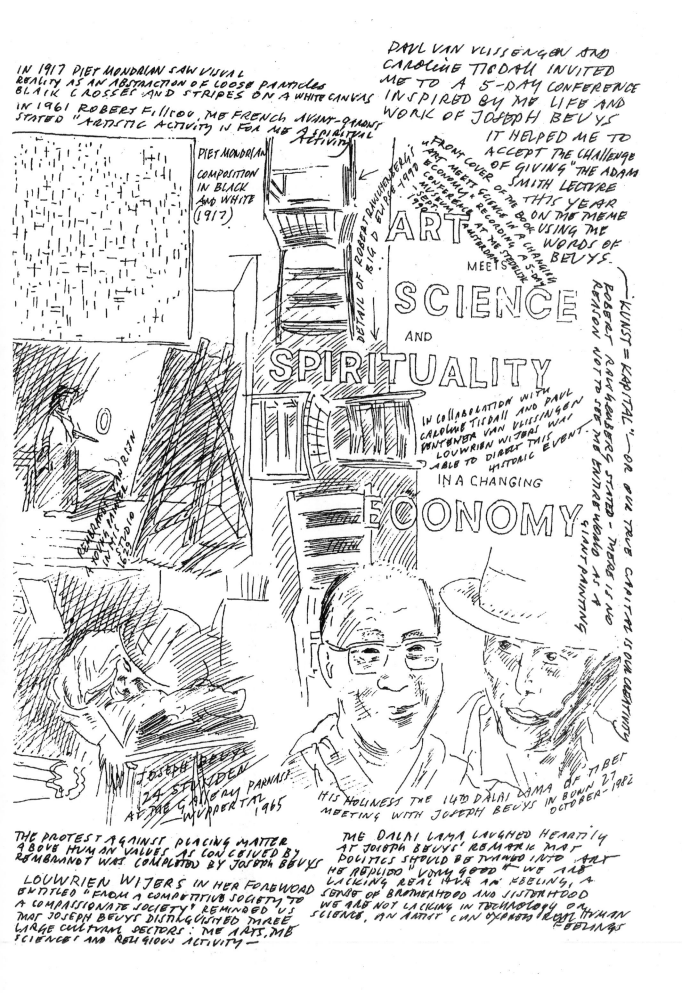

IN 1917 PIET MONDRIAN SAW VISUAL
REALITY AS AN ABSTRACTION OF LOOSE PARTICLES
BLACK CROSSES AND STRIPES ON A WHITE CANVAS
IN 1961 ROBERT FILLIOU, THE FRENCH AVANT-GARDIST
STATED "ARTISTIC ACTIVITY IS FOR ME A SPIRITUAL
Activity"

PIET MONDRIAN
COMPOSITION
IN BLACK
AND WHITE
(1917)

PAUL VAN VLISSINGEN AND
CAROLINE TISDALL INVITED
ME TO A 5-DAY CONFERENCE
INSPIRED BY THE LIFE AND
WORK OF JOSEPH BEUYS

IT HELPED ME TO
ACCEPT THE CHALLENGE
OF GIVING "THE ADAM
SMITH LECTURE
THIS YEAR
ON THE THEME
USING THE
WORDS OF
BEUYS.

DETAIL OF BIG D EU PGE 1990 ROBERT RAUSCHENBERG'S

"FRONT COVER OF THE BOOK
ART MEETS SCIENCE IN A CHANGING
ECONOMY + RECORDING A 5-DAY
CONFERENCE AT THE STEDELIJK
MUSEUM AMSTERDAM SEPT.
1990.

ART

MEETS

SCIENCE

AND

SPIRITUALITY

IN COLLABORATION WITH
CAROLINE TISDALL AND PAUL
FENTENER VAN VLISSINGEN
LOUWRIEN WIJERS WAS
ABLE TO DIRECT THIS
HISTORIC EVENT.

IN A CHANGING

ECONOMY

"KUNST = KAPITAL" — OR OUR TRUE CAPITAL IS OUR CREATIVITY
ROBERT RAUSCHENBERG STATED — THERE IS NO
REASON NOT TO SEE THE ENTIRE WORLD AS A
GIANT PAINTING

REMBRANDT THE RISEN
YOUNG PAINTER
1629-1010

JOSEPH BEUYS
24 STUNDEN
AT THE GALLERY PARNASS
WUPPERTAL 1965

HIS HOLINESS THE 14TH DALAI LAMA OF TIBET
MEETING WITH JOSEPH BEUYS IN BONN 27
OCTOBER 1982

THE PROTEST AGAINST PLACING MATTER
ABOVE HUMAN VALUES AS CONCEIVED BY
REMBRANDT WAS COMPLETED BY JOSEPH BEUYS

LOUWRIEN WIJERS IN HER FOREWORD
ENTITLED "FROM A COMPETITIVE SOCIETY TO
A COMPASSIONATE SOCIETY' REMINDED US
THAT JOSEPH BEUYS DISTINGUISHED THREE
LARGE CULTURAL SECTORS: THE ARTS, THE
SCIENCES AND RELIGIOUS ACTIVITY —

THE DALAI LAMA LAUGHED HEARTILY
AT JOSEPH BEUYS' REMARK THAT
POLITICS SHOULD BE TURNED INTO ART
HE REPLIED "VERY GOOD + WE ARE
LACKING REAL HUMAN FEELING, A
SENSE OF BROTHERHOOD AND SISTERHOOD
WE ARE NOT LACKING IN TECHNOLOGY OR
SCIENCE, AN ARTIST CAN EXPRESS REAL HUMAN
FEELINGS

In an issue of the magazine *Scottish International Review* published in 1968 Cordelia Oliver, then Northern Art critic of the *Guardian,* put the question, "What is the Richard Demarco Gallery attempting to do? And in any case do we really need it?"

I would rephrase the question thus: "If there were no Demarco Gallery would it be necessary to create one?"

This really means does Scotland need a gallery which has the intention of earning for itself an international reputation, and does it need a gallery which can vie with the most established galleries on Madison Avenue or the Rue St. Honoré.

It is reassuring that an artist of the stature of Patrick Heron should say of the exhibition space which the Demarco Gallery provides: "It is as splendid a setting for modern painting as any private gallery, and British artists should be queueing up to exhibit there."

Cordelia Oliver, as someone intimately concerned with the devlopment of the visual arts in Scotland, pointed out rightly that the Demarco Gallery's function is to support every activity which already sells Scottish art to Scottish patrons, but it is surely incredible that there has not been a gallery until recently with the primary aims of internationalising the world in which Scottish artists normally operate.

Why has there been almost no opportunity for Scotland's artists to have a share of the limelight on the international stage within the kind of setting provided by the Venice Biennale or Documenta?

Is it because nobody has been prepared to spend the money or make the effort to create contacts with those who organise these exhibitions?

Why is Britain usually represented by artists working in and around London?

It is difficult to believe that I was perhaps the first Scot to be officially asked to the openings of the Venice Biennale and the Documenta as a representative of a prize-winning artist.

It did seem even to me unlikely that an Edinburgh Art Gallery should be representing a Colombian artist – the sculptor Edgar Negret. Surely the next step is for a Scottish artist to be thus represented?

The policy of the Demarco Gallery is not to ignore the work of Scottish artists but on the contrary to prove that Scotland has confidence in its artists competing on an international level.

The Edinburgh Open 100 and Canada 101 were two exhibitions born out of the spirit of the Demarco Gallery. They proved that the Edinburgh Festival can present contemporary painting alongside the best contemporary music and drama. Suddenly Sassenach artists were obliged to focus their attention on Scotland.

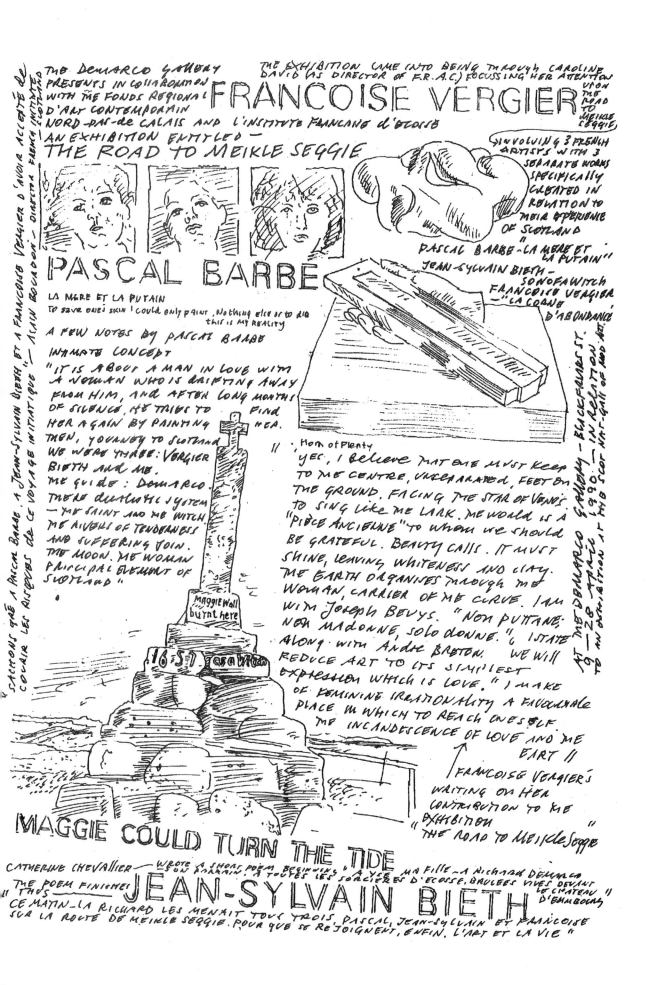

THE DEMARCO GALLERY PRESENTS IN COLLABORATION WITH THE FONDS REGIONAL D'ART CONTEMPORAIN NORD-PAS-de CALAIS AND L'INSTITUTE FRANCAIS d'ECOSSE AN EXHIBITION ENTITLED—

THE EXHIBITION CAME INTO BEING THROUGH CAROLINE DAVID (AS DIRECTOR OF F.R.A.C.) FOCUSSING HER ATTENTION UPON THE ROAD TO MEIKLE SEGGIE.

FRANCOISE VERGIER

THE ROAD TO MEIKLE SEGGIE

(INVOLVING 3 FRENCH ARTISTS WITH 3 SEPARATE WORKS SPECIFICALLY CREATED IN RELATION TO THEIR EXPERIENCE OF SCOTLAND)

PASCAL BARBE-"LA MERE ET LA PUTAIN"

JEAN-SYLVAIN BIETH— SONOFAWITCH

FRANCOISE VERGIER—"LA CORNE D'ABONDANCE"

PASCAL BARBE

LA MERE ET LA PUTAIN

"To save one's skin I could only paint, nothing else or to die this is my reality"

A FEW NOTES BY PASCAL BARBE

INNATE CONCEPT

"IT IS ABOUT A MAN IN LOVE WITH A WOMAN WHO IS DRIFTING AWAY FROM HIM, AND AFTER LONG MONTHS OF SILENCE, HE TRIES TO FIND HER AGAIN BY PAINTING HER. THEN, YOU JOURNEY TO SCOTLAND WE WERE THREE: VERGIER BIETH AND ME. THE GUIDE: DEMARCO. THERE DUALISTIC SYSTEM — THE SAINT AND THE WITCH THE RIVERS OF TENDERNESS AND SUFFERING JOIN. THE MOON. THE WOMAN PRINCIPAL ELEMENT OF SCOTLAND"

Horn of Plenty

Maggie Wall burnt here

1657 as a witch

YES, I BELIEVE THAT ONE MUST KEEP TO THE CENTRE, UNSEPARATED, FEET ON THE GROUND. FACING THE STAR OF VENUS TO SING LIKE THE LARK. THE WORLD IS A "PIECE ANCIENNE" TO WHOM WE SHOULD BE GRATEFUL. BEAUTY CALLS. IT MUST SHINE, LEAVING WHITENESS AND CLAY. THE EARTH ORGANISES THROUGH THE WOMAN, CARRIER OF THE CURVE. I AM WITH Joseph BEUYS. "Non PUTTANE, NON MADONNE, SOLO DONNE." I STATE ALONG WITH André BRETON. WE WILL REDUCE ART TO ITS SIMPLEST EXPRESSION WHICH IS LOVE." I MAKE OF FEMININE IRRATIONALITY A FAVOURABLE PLACE IN WHICH TO REACH ONESELF THE INCANDESCENCE OF LOVE AND THE EARTH //

FRANCOISE VERGIER'S WRITING ON HER CONTRIBUTION TO THE "EXHIBITION" THE ROAD TO MEIKLE SEGGIE

AT THE DEMARCO GALLERY — BLACKFRIARS ST. 9 - 28 APRIL 1990 - IN RELATION TO AN EXHIBITION AT THE SCOT NAT. GALL OF MOD. ART.

"SACHONS QUE A PASCAL BARBE, A JEAN-SYLVAIN BIETH ET A FRANCOISE VERGIER D'AVOIR ACCEPTÉ DE COURIR LES RISQUES DE CE VOYAGE INITIATIQUE" — ALAIN BOUDON— DIRECTA FIENC INITITUTE d'ECOSSE

MAGGIE COULD TURN THE TIDE

CATHERINE CHEVALLIER— WROTE A SHORT POEM BEGINNING "SON REFRAIN A TOUTES LES SORCIERES D'ECOSSE, BRULEES VIVES DEVANT LE CHATEAU D'EDIMBOURG
THE POEM FINISHED "THUS

JEAN-SYLVAIN BIETH

A YSE MA FILLE—A RICHARD DEMARCO

CE MATIN-LA RICHARD LES MENAIT TOUS TROIS, PASCAL, JEAN-SYLVAIN ET FRANCOISE SUR LA ROUTE DE MEIKLE SEGGIE. POUR QUE SE REJOIGNENT, ENFIN, L'ART ET LA VIE"

The disappearance without human trace of the Picts, those once worthy and fearsome enemies of the Roman Legions, who dared to venture northwards on The Road to Meikle Seggie from the line of the Antonine Wall, the final north western frontier of the Roman Empire, is the one of the great mysteries of European history. The Roman dreams of conquest were shattered at the Battle of Mons Graupius, and the legend of the Lost Legion was created in the footsteps of the Roman Legionaries. Later came the Christian missionaries, some from the Mediterranean, such as St Servanus, known today in Scotland as St Serf, he who killed the Dragon of Dunning, and those who came from 'Scot-Land', the land of the 'Irish', followers of Saints Patrick and Columba. Outstanding among them was St Fillan.

Their missionary journeys are recorded in important place names on the Road to Meikle Seggie; Inch Colum (the Island of St Columba),

St Serf's Cave at Pittenweem. The Firth of Forth was the historic river estuary which directed them to and from the European continent – that is why there is an inevitability in discovering St Fillan's Church next door to Charlemagne's Imperial Chapel at Aachen, and why Moenchengladbach means 'The Place of Irish Monks' and why St Gallen in Switzerland is identified as a centre of Celtic Christianity.

Gunther Uecker's map of Europe naturally focuses upon such locations of intense spiritual energy. That is why it is perfectly normal that he should have a major exhibition in St Gallen.

It is typical of Gunther Uecker's never-ending search for the cultural origins of the Europe he loves so passionately, that his exhibition 'Pictlandgarden' should set him on a personal quest never before considered by any contemporary artist with the necessary skill and commitment to re-invigorate the meaning of Pictish culture in the context of the New Europe.

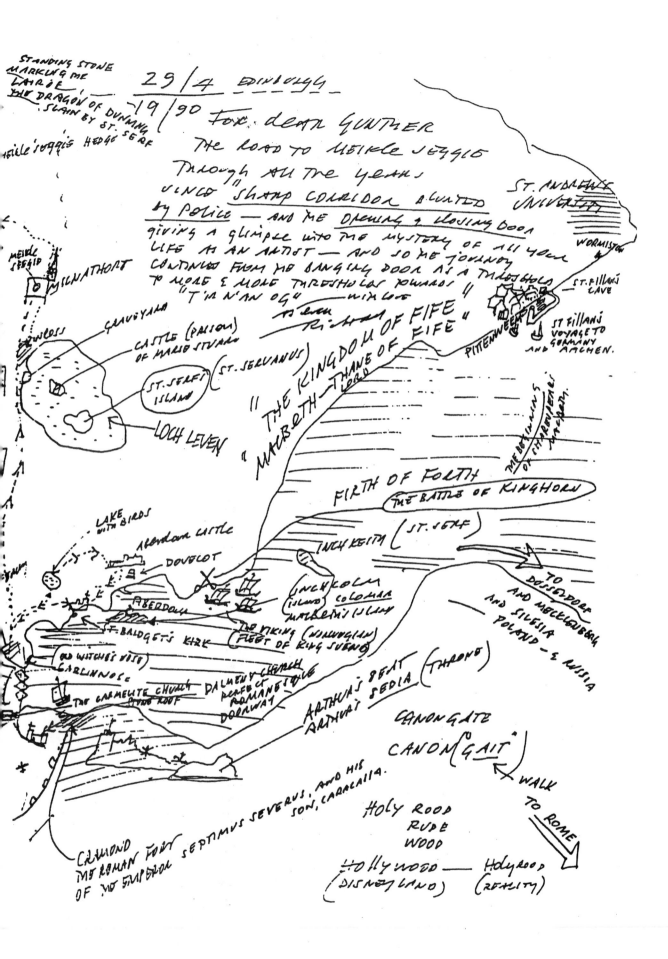

STANDING STONE
MARKING THE
LAIRDE
THE DRAGON OF DUNMNG
SLAIN BY ST. SERF

MEIKLE SEGGIE HEDGE

29/4 EDINBURGH
19/90 FOR. DEAR GUNTHER

THE ROAD TO MEIKLE SEGGIE
THROUGH ALL THE YEARS
SINCE "SHARP CORRIDOR ALERTED
BY POLICE — AND THE OPENING & CLOSING DOOR
GIVING A GLIMPSE INTO THE MYSTERY OF ALL YOUR
LIFE AS AN ARTIST — AND SO THE JOURNEY
CONTINUES FROM THE BANGING DOOR AS A THRESHOLD
TO MORE & MORE THRESHOLDS TOWARDS
"TIR N'AN OG" — WITH LOVE

ST. ANDREWS
UNIVERSITY

WORMISTON

ST FILLANS
CAVE

ST FILLANS
VOYAGE TO
GERMANY
AACHEN.

TO EVEN
Richard

MEIKLE
SEGGIE

MILNATHORT

GRAVEYARD

CASTLE (PRISON)
OF MARIE STUART

ST. SERF
ISLAND

(ST. SERVANUS)

"THE KINGDOM OF FIFE"

"MACBETH—THANE OF FIFE"

PITENWEEM

LORD

THE BEGINNINGS
OF CHRISTENDOM? IN-REAL

LOCH LEVEN

LAKE
WITH BIRDS

ABERDOUR CASTLE

DOVECOT

INCHKEITH

(ST. SERF)

FIRTH OF FORTH

THE BATTLE OF KINGHORN

TO
DÜSSELDORF
AND MECKLENBURG
AND SILESIA
POLAND—& RUSSIA

INCHCOLM
ISLAND COLUMBA
MACBETH'S ISLAND

ABERDOUR

T. BALDGET'S KIRK

THE VIKING (NORWEGIAN)
FLEET OF KING SUENO

OLD WITCH'S WIFE
CARLINNOSE

THE CARMELITE CHURCH
STONE ROOF

DALMENY CHURCH
PERFECT
ROMANESQUE
DOORWAY

ARTHUR'S SEAT
ARTHUR'S SEDIA (THRONE)

CANONGATE
CANON(GAIT'

WALK

CRAMOND
THE ROMAN FORT
OF THE EMPEROR SEPTIMUS SEVERUS, AND HIS
SON, CARACALLA.

HOLY ROOD
RUDE
WOOD

Hollywood — Holyrood
(DISNEYLAND)   (REALITY)

TO ROME

Gunther Uecker and Joseph Beuys had much in common and it seemed entirely appropriate that soon after 'Strategy-Get-Arts' I should find myself compelled to visit Stockholm, where Pontus Hulten had established himself as the most innovative museum director imaginable.

In his wisdom, and with his usual sense of good timing, he had organised an exhibition dedicated entirely to the significance of Gunther Uecker and Joseph Beuys, as outstanding examples of artists capable of helping Europe to regain a sense of its true cultural identity.

In Scotland, through the song and poetry of a Celtic people, such journeyings inevitably lead to what they have always known as Tir na Nog – 'The Land of the Ever Young' which lies beyond the midsummer sun's setting over the limitless spaces of the Western Atlantic Ocean.

Gunther Uecker and his wife, Christine, and their son, Jacob, discovered together the quintessential experience of this landscape and seascape in the Inner Hebridean Island world of Colin Lindsay MacDougall, whose Lungha estates incorporated the Firth of Lorne. The MacDougalls have been there for over 800 years claiming a proud heritage from those Lords of the Isles whose galleys could help provide a fleet of 600 ships, strong enough to patrol their domain, stretching from the Isle of Man to Dublin Bay, from the coast of Ulster towards the Western Isles.

From the windows of Lungha castle can be seen the Paps of Jura, and the uninhabited island mass of Scarba and the swirling of the Correyvreckan, the largest and most frightening whirlpool in all of Europe.

To reach this Celtic world, Gunther Uecker had to traverse the heartland of the Picts which lies north and west of the Firth of Forth. When I first met him, in 1967, at the first ever exhibition of ROSC in Dublin, I had wanted him to know that the Celtic world that he had discovered in Ireland had a different connotation in Scotland, when considered alongside the culture of the Picts who, inextricably linked with the Celts, and every bit as interesting, managed to remain comparatively unknown to the world at large.

ROSC 1967 was, of course, the perfect place in which to meet Gunther Uecker, because complementary to the exhibition of contemporary art works was the exhibition of Celtic treasures from the treasure house of Ireland's national museum. In ROSC 1967, the uncompromising present and future of Europe was thus identified with Europe's remote past, through the mysterious but enduring identity of the Celts.

The Celts are recognisable today in the faces and activities of the Irish people, in the poetry of their thought and speech and, of course, in Scotland's West Highlanders and Islanders, those descendants of the Lords of the Isles, whose territory joined together Scotland and Ireland. The Pictish lands did not reach Ireland, and it is much more difficult to recognise the way in which they make themselves manifest today, because their language and the sound of their voices have gone forever.

154/

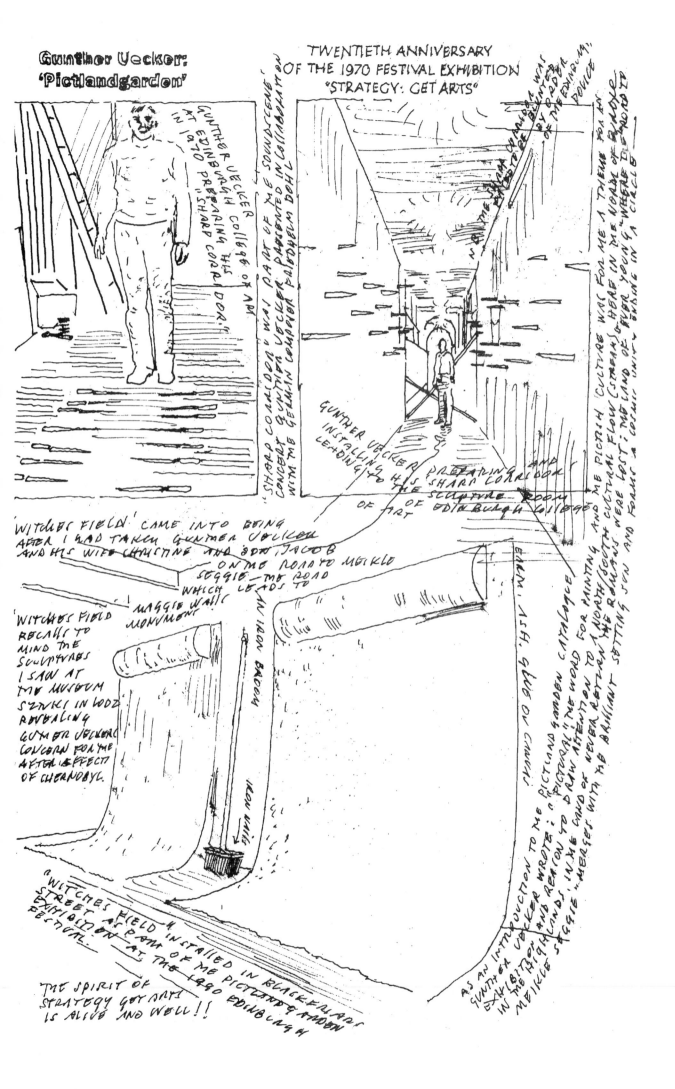

Gunther Uecker: 'Pictlandgarden'

GUNTHER UECKER AT EDINBURGH COLLEGE OF ART IN 1970 PREPARING HIS "SHARP CORRIDOR"

"SHARP CORRIDOR" IS PART OF THE SOUNDSCENE CONCEPT GUNTHER UECKER PRESENTED IN COLLABORATION WITH THE GERMAN COMPOSER FRIEDHELM DÖHL

GUNTHER UECKER INSTALLING HIS LEADING TO THE SCULPTURE ROOM

PREPARING HIS SHARP CORRIDOR OF OF ART EDINBURGH COLLEGE

THE SCULPTURE ROOM ORANGE WAS PAINTED BY ORDER OF THE EDINBURGH POLICE

ON THE PICTISH CULTURE WAS FOR ME A THEME FOR AN EXHIBITION CULTURAL FLOW STREAMS HERE IN THE NORTH OF THE NORTH/SOUTH ROADS WERE LOST; THE LAND OF EVER YOUNG — WHERE THE SOLID & THE LAND OF FANUS A COSMIC UNITY ENDING IN A CIRCLE

'WITCHES FIELD' CAME INTO BEING AFTER I HAD TAKEN GUNTHER UECKER AND HIS WIFE CHRISTINE AND SON JACOB ON THE ROAD TO MEIKLE SEGGIE — THE ROAD WHICH LEADS TO MAGGIE WALLS MONUMENT

'WITCHES FIELD' RECALLS TO MIND THE SCULPTURES I SAW AT THE MUSEUM SZTUKI IN LODZ REVEALING GUNTHER UECKER CONCERN FOR THE AFTER EFFECTS OF CHERNOBYL.

AN IRON BADGE

IRON NAILS

AS AN INTRODUCTION TO THE PICTLAND GARDEN CATALOGUE GUNTHER UECKER WROTE: A PICTORIAL THE WORD FOR PAINTING AND REASON TO DRAW ATTENTION TO A NORTH EXHIBITION IN THE HIGHLANDS. IN THE LAND OF NEVER RETURN THE ROADS SETTING SUN AND FANUS MEIKLE SEGGIE — MERGES WITH THE BRILLIANT

ENEM., ASH, GLUE ON CANVAS

"WITCHES FIELD" INSTALLED IN BLACKFRIARS STREET AS PART OF THE PICTLAND GARDEN EXHIBITION AT THE 1990 EDINBURGH FESTIVAL.

THE SPIRIT OF 'STRATEGY GET ARTS' IS ALIVE AND WELL!!

My attendance at conferences on the subject of Art and Science presented by 'Interalia' at the Royal Botanic Garden in Edinburgh inspired by the polymath Professor D'Arcy Thomson and his seminal book 'Growth and Form' and my lecture to The Royal Philosophical Society of Glasgow at their annual dinner has further encouraged me consider ways in which the interface between art and science can be explored through the arts and science faculties at Kingston as a model for the future of University education in Europe.

The Baltic Conference presented in Dundee at Discovery Point by Scottish Enterprise, Tayside enabled me to deliver an address to all the delegates representing Estonia, Latvia and Lithuania in dialogue with Scotland and to discuss the need for bringing up-to-date the fruitful and historic spirit of the Hanseatic League. It ended with dinner in Captain Scott's ship **The Discovery** the twelve speakers hosted by Lord Dundee, the Patron of the Conference with Vytautis Landsbergis as the Guest of Honour, giving everyone the benefit of his wisdom and experience as a politician and artist.

This conference enabled me to give a message from Professor Richard Ennals to all the speakers and delegates outlining the work that he and his father, Lord Ennals, have been involved in to link not only Kingston with Vilnius University, but Lithuania with Britain.

Now that Lord Gowrie with his renowned interest in the culture of Eastern Europe has replaced Lord Palumbo as Chairman of the Arts Council, I hope to bring up to date the work which I have been privileged to carry out with his support in creating cultural dialogues between Britain and Eastern Europe – particularly Poland, Russia and Hungary.

THE BURNING OF 'LOCAL HERO'
TOOK PLACE IN BLACKFRIARS STREET
BEFORE THE GALLERY-GOERS WHO
HAD BEEN INVITED TO ATTEND
THE OPENING OF
THE
GALLERY;
FESTIVAL
EXHIBITION

THE ELEMENTARY FORCES OF
FIRE AND WATER WERE CONJOINED
THE UMBRELLA INDICATES
THE ACTION
TOOK PLACE IN
A DOWNPOUR OF
RAIN

THE MAKING OF THE SCULPTURE AND THE ACTION"
(PERFORMED BY DAVID MACH TOGETHER WITH THE BURNING OF
PART OF KINGSTON UNIVERSITY'S CONTRIBUTION TO THE 1992 DEMARCO GALLERY
EDINBURGH FESTIVAL EXHIBITION ENTITLED "PENTAGONATE PLUS"

WHICH BURNED, WAS
COMBINED WITH THIS BECAME "AND THE FICTION"

ROBERT MACH

DAVID MACH

'LOCAL HERO' WAS THE NAME GIVEN BY DAVID MACH
TO HIS SCULPTURE MADE OF THOUSANDS OF MATCHES. BY THE
PROCESS OF SETTING IT ALIGHT, THE BRIGHTLY COLOURED HEAD
WAS ENVELOPED IN FLAMES FOR A FEW MINUTES THEN EMERGED
A BLACKENED MASK, REMINISCENT OF AFRICAN MASKS.
IT WAS A PORTRAIT OF MYSELF AS I ENDED MY DAYS AS DIRECTOR
OF THE DEMARCO GALLERY IN BLACKFRIARS STREET

Richard DEMARCO

The most spectacular space of the gallery's theatre was undoubtedly that of Inchcolm Island, together with the good ship **Maid of the Forth,** both providing settings for John Bett's spectacular 1989 production of Shakcspeare's Macbeth with Scottish actors, giving a new meaning to the play literally within the domain of the Thane of Fife and his wife. John Bett was given but twelve days to create his masterwork. Who will ever forget the rain driving against the throne and crown of Macbeth, played con bravura by John Cairney as he confronts Macduff to learn that his reign of terror is at an end, as the sun set spectacularly over the Forth Bridge, and the moon rose over Edinburgh Castle four miles distant across the waters of the Forth? Roy Hanlon gave a bravura performance as the Porter, as did Gerda Stevenson as Lady Macbeth. Eric Ibler, as director of music, for the production and chorus master of Edinburgh's Schola Cantorum, orchestrated a musical element which evoked the authentic sounds you would expect to have heard from medieval monks at prayer in Inchcolm Abbey.

It followed the 1988 production of La Zattera Di Babele – the Rome and Sicily based Company of Carlo Quartucci and Carla Tato. Their production of The Scottish Play brought together the sound of both the Italian and English languages. John Bett and Juliet Cadzow made sure the sound of English was suitably Scottish in accent. This production brought together the basic principles of classic theatre and performance art. It began at the Demarco Gallery, continued by bus journey and sea voyage to end at Inchcolm, a production which hit an operatic high note with the recorded sound of Verdi's *Macbeth* and linked not only the official Festival with the Fringe, but also every imaginable use of contemporary dance, music, acting, performance art and even sculpture of the highest quality associated with Jannis Kouncllis and Giulio Paolini, two of the Italian avant-garde artists prepared to work with La Zattera Di Babele through Rudi Fuchs, Director of the now legendary Documenta Seven, in itself questioning the normal definitions implied by the words 'gallery' or 'theatre'.

This Italo-Scottish production was enlarged upon when it was presented literally above cloud-level in the precipitous mountain-top Sicilian town of Erice, in a world seemingly inhabited by Greek. and Roman deities.

AMONG THE PARTICIPANTS JANE HAD TO CONSIDER WERE BRYANDIS SNAEBJORNSDOTTIR - PATRICIA DOLKHWAITE - ROSE FLAIN - CLARE THACKER (WHO WAS DIRECTING EDINBURGH ARTS PERFORMANCES INVOLVING HER FELLOW PARTICIPANTS) ANNE SEAGRAVE WAS ALSO A PERFORMANCE ARTIST WHO WAS MAKING SOLO PERFORMANCES. EDINBURGH ANTERS EXPERIENCED WORE MANICFULLY MOVE TO HELP - TERRY NEWMAN AND SALLY DUNSMORE, JANE CHISHOLM, ANNE GORLING

THANKFULLY THE PROGRAMME IN WROCLAW WAS IN THE CAPABLE HANDS OF OLD AND TRUSTY FRIENDS — THE POLISH ARTISTS ZBIGNIEW MAKAROWICZ AND BARBARA KOSLOWSKA WHO WERE ALSO DIRECTING GALLERY "X". ZBIGNIEW WAS ALSO THE PRESIDENT OF THE Polish UNION OF ARTISTS

THERE WERE 33 PARTICIPANTS IN ALL.

JANE MacALLISTER IN CONTEMPLATIVE MOOD ENJOYING A MOMENT OF PEACE AFTER DINNER IN WROCLAW WHILST ON THE 1990 EDINBURGH ARTS EXPEDITION TO POLAND. AS USUAL ON THESE EXPEDITIONS SHE HAD THE NOWHALE TASK OF DEALING WITH THE DAILY PROGRAMME AND THE NEEDS OF THE ARTISTS WE WERE MEETING — TEN YEARS OF "EDINBURGH ARTS" TRAVELS HAD MADE HER INVALUABLE AS THE "ARTIST AS EXPLORER"

In its 25th anniversary year in 1991, the Demarco Gallery focused all its energies on the concept of Pentagonale, originating in the political strategies of Italy's Minister of Foreign Affairs, Gianni di Michaelis. It was his political acumen and his support of the European Community which brought Pentagonale into being as a political, economic, scientific and cultural Pan-European community, it was designed to bring Italy closer to Austria, Hungary, and the former states of Czechoslovakia and Yugoslavia. Poland joined to make it Pentagonale-Plus – with Romania and Bulgaria still waiting patiently to follow Poland's example. The 1991 Demarco Gallery's exhibition and theatre programme was therefore possessed of a very distinct Italian, Austrian, Hungarian, Czechoslovak, Polish, Yugoslav, Romanian and Bulgarian mixture, suggesting that the Demarco Gallery's future lay very much in what could be seen as Europe's new heartland.

The Italian contribution to the Pentagonale-Plus programme questioned the very idea that a theatrical performance needs to be presented in a clearly designated theatre space. The Laboratorio Teatre Settimo from Turin, consisting of four actors, devised their work entitled Stabat Mater so that it had to be performed in the domestic setting of a house or flat. Their performances ended with the performers preparing coffee for the audience. I was indebted to Nina Mehta for persuading them to perform as part of the Gallery's commitment to the concept of Pentagonale. She recognised them as being representative of that creative spirit which so successfully animates those Italian artists with whom she had been in fruitful dialogue in Italy over a period of seven months in 1990 – from the contemporaries of 1950's avant-gardists like the 73 year old Mimmo Rotella, to recent art 'school graduates such as 23 year old Francesco Chiais, and the directors and actors of Milan's Out-Off theatre.

LITTLE DID I IMAGINE WHEN I DREW THIS IMAGE OF
ST ANDREWS THAT I WOULD BE ASKED BY ST. ANDREWS
UNIVERSITY STUDENTS TO RUN IN THEIR RECTORIAL
ELECTION IN 1991. AUBERON WAUGH AND
GLENDA JACKSON WERE AMONG THE SEVEN
CONTENDERS. I FOUND MYSELF AS
RUNNER-UP TO NICHOLAS PARSONS

THIS DRAWING RESULTED FROM MY COMMISSION.
I RECEIVED FROM THE OLD COURSE HOTEL TO PAINT
A 60-FOOT LONG MURAL FOR THE CORRIDOR LEADING
TO THE HOTEL RESTAURANT — WHEN A JAPANESE
MULTIMILLIONAIRE BUSINESS MAN CALLED HAMADA SAN
VISITED THE HOTEL HE COMMISSIONED A JAPANESE
FOR THE HOTEL. HE ENVISIONED A HAMADA MURAL
COMPLETE HIS PLANS FOR THE
JAPANESE REPLICA OF THE
OLD COURSE ITSELF.

18 TH HOLE, THE OLD COURSE, ST. ANDREWS   Richard Demarco 68

1991 ended with the news of Tadeusz Kantor's untimely death. His presence is still sorely missed, but thankfully, there are bittersweet memories of his Cricot II actors who performed last year in the newly reopened Empire Theatre. Their production of *Today is My Birthday,* in aid of the Demarco Gallery East Europe Art Foundation, was a triumphant theatrical event even without his presence.

It was comforting to see the Cricot Company in the Demarco Gallery, after their performance, enjoying the extraordinary film made by Gabriella Cardazzo and Duncan Ward. The film was in every sense celebratory, revealing Kantor's capacity to express the genius of the Christo-Judaic tradition of art-making which was at the heart of the gallery's 25th Anniversary Exhibition and conference – Pentagonale Plus, and which brought Gianni De Michelis as Italy's Foreign Minister to the Edinburgh Festival and enabled me to spend a memorable day with Jack Lang as Minister of Culture of France on the Road to Meikle Seggie, the road which leads the gallery inevitably into the New Europe.

In 1992, Paulina Kolczynska, Anya Kemalow and Pawel Frelik represent the Polish aspects of the gallery's festival programme. Krzysztof Borowlee and Jerzy Luzynski are bringing back to Edinburgh their unforgettable Polish-Russian Grupa Chwilowa with *A Stop in the Desert,* with two of Moscow's leading actors, Aleksiej Zajcev and Irina Nabatova, who enchanted Edinburgh Festival goers in 1991 with arguably the most compelling piece of theatre worthy of a comparison with Tadeusz Kantor's Cricot II Theatre.

Grupa Chwilowa should not be missed, and neither should the new production of Lotte-Lachmann Theatre Operation 'Alcestis'.

Neither should the Poznan Dance Company, probably the most ingenious and creative exponents of ballet to be found in all of Eastern Europe – as well as Teatr 77 from Lodz, and Lublin's compelling Teatr Provisorium.

Robert Ferguson's gravestone
Canongate Churchyard

1992 is the year in which I found myself, to my astonishment, the recipient of the Award of the British Centre of the International Theatre Institute. The award was celebrated at a delightful luncheon at the Garrick Club, and to my delight was presented by Richard Eyre, not just as Director of the National Theatre, but as a veteran of the Edinburgh Festival from his days at Edinburgh's Lyceum Theatre. We were able to reminisce about Tadeusz Kantor's first ever production in the world of English-speaking theatre at the Poorhouse, Forresthill, when Richard Eyre, as the *Scotsman's* Theatre Critic, was the first to write in unstinted praise of Kantor's genius.

Little did either of us know that on that same day of celebration on April 27, the International Theatre Day, the Polish Centre of the International Theatre Institute had also decided to give its award, to what I must consider to be all those dedicated souls who have put their considerable effort into helping me transform the Demarco Gallery for the past seven years at Festival time, into a stage and testing-ground for international theatre.

Our programme has come to be expressed with emphasis on a distinct East European tradition, inspired by the world Stanislaw Witkiewicz committed himself to between the two World Wars. The Polish International Theatre Prize was therefore aptly named the Witkiewicz Prize

The Polish Award enabled me to spend seven days in Poland, searching out new aspects of Polish theatre which augur well for future Edinburgh Festival Programmes of Demarco Gallery Theatre, and in the process observe the Poznan Dance Theatre in performance on the largest stage in Europe – in Warsaw's Opera House.

I was also witness to an extraordinary evocation of the world of James Joyce's Dublin, performed by the company of actors directed by Henryk Baranowski. Focused upon Molly Bloom's soliloquy, the play is entitled *Yes, I will, yes*. Molly Bloom is performed by Monika Niemczyk, an actress of outstanding ability, who managed to convey the unutterable Irishness of Molly Bloom's spirit – not only in her physical appearance, but in the very sound and rhythm of her voice, so that her Polish language embodied the quintessential music of Joyce's words.

Richard Demarco '92   THE HOUSE OF THE SISTER OF
                                       TOBIAS SMOLLETT

Janusz Wisniewski as director of its own eponymous theatre company, now housed in a converted cinema in Szwedzka Street in the Praga district of Warsaw's East Bank, enabled me to see the final dress rehearsal of his latest work which, translated, is entitled *Wonderful Life*. It is full of ironic images of the present European turmoil. It was Janusz Wisniewski who presented me with the Witkiewicz Prize in the Ateacura Theatre which is also the office of the Polish Centre of the International Theatre Institute. As an artist as well as a man of theatre, Janusz Wisniewski had actually designed the award in the form of one of his paintings.

The director of the institute, Janusz Warminski, spoke of his happy memories of the 1963 Edinburgh Writers' Conference to the 60 representatives of the Polish theatre world who attended the ceremony and reminded me that among the Polish delegation was Zbigniew Cybulski, the Polish film actor and star of *Ashes and Diamonds*. He refreshed my own memories of the Polish 'James Dean' who seemed always to wear dark sunglasses throughout his stay in Edinburgh.

In response to these awards, it seemed necessary and entirely appropriate to strike a note of celebration with a 1992 theatre programme which would mark the end of a chapter in the gallery's 26-year-life, a chapter closing the seven-year period when the gallery enjoyed the use of a building which must surely be, by its very beauty and capacity to inspire artists, actors, musicians and dancers, the ideal space which the founders of the Traverse would have gladly contemplated if they had but known of its existence – a multi-purpose space for all the arts, a house for artists, a living and working space.

It is a sad and perplexing thought that such an ideal building never attracted the public funding it surely deserved, but thankfully it will do so in the future, when that much-needed funding will come from the Italian Government, when the building is transformed into what must surely be the ideal of an Italian Cultural Institute. As such, it should continue to attract attention from all those who take seriously the map defining the cultural life of the New Europe, with Edinburgh and its historic Old Town as a focal point at the heart and centre of the Festival. The gallery is planning to establish its East Europe Art Foundation Office as close as possible to 17-21 Blackfriars Street. This office should also enable work to be carried out on the Demarco Oallery's archive.

The Demarco Gallery and Theatre, under the aegis of the East Europe Art Foundation will doubtless re-establish itself with a programme dedicated to the development of the visual and performing arts in the New Europe for the 3-week period of next year's Festival, and hopefully those to follow leading to the New Millennium.

the Estonian Youth Theatre

ROMEO

AND JULIET

OR TO DUNDEE — OR AGAIN CLOUGH?

CAN I BRING THE ESTONIAN YOUTH THEATRE BACK TO EDINBURGH?

KIERKEGAARD

AT LITTLE SPARTA AS PART OF THE GARDEN ROUTE TO THE EDINBURGH FESTIVAL.

AND PERFORMED AT DUNDEE REP. DIRECTED BY SUE POSSER

ALL WOMEN AND QUITE A FEW WOMEN ARE RIGHT, ACCORDING TO ROGER POOLE'S PLAY INSPIRED BY SOLEN KIERKEGAARD'S LOVE FOR REGINE OLSEN.

THE PLAY READING WAS AT "LITTLE SPARTA" AT THE INVITATION OF IAN HAMILTON FINLAY.

THE EUROPEAN YOUTH
PARLIAMENT'S SESSION
IN STRASBOURG IN JULY
1992 CONTAINED WITHIN
IT AN EXPERIMENT IN ART
EDUCATION DEFINING THE
SPIRIT OF THE NEW EUROPE
THE DEMARCO EUROPEAN
ART FOUNDATION AWARDED
SCHOLARSHIPS TO ALL THE
STUDENTS INVOLVED
IN THE PARLIAMENTS
TWO SESSIONS IN
STRASBOURG
AND IN GHENT
THE ART ACADEMIES
OF STRASBOURG AND
GHENT PROVIDED
THE PRINT MAKING
FACILITIES AND STAFF
WHO COLLABORATED
WITH ARTHUR WATSON
AND MARY MODEEN
AS MASTER-PRINTER-
TEACHERS.

THE ART STUDENTS WHO WORKED AT
L'ECOLE DES ARTS DECORATIFS, STRASBOURG
WERE : NIEDJELKO MIKAC (CROATIA)-
AKADEMIJA LIKOVVIH·ZAGREB
IAN WILEY (ENGLAND) KINGSTON
ANNE WICKEY (FRANCE) STRASBOURG
AGOTA KORNYEI (HUNGARY) ACAD OF FINE ARTS
                                    BUDAPEST
DANIELA D'ALLORA (ITALY) ACCADEMIA VENICE
ARUNAS GELUNAS (LITHUANIA) ART ACADEMY. VILNUS
KAREN VAUGHAN (NORTHERN IRELAND) SCHOOL OF ART
UNIVERSITY OF ULSTER. BELFAST
CARL HANSEN (NORWAY) VESTLANDETS
KUNSTAKADEMI BERGEN
ARTUR WOJTCZUK. ART ACADEMY, WARSAW
ALEXANDER, DIEGO LOPES. ANTONIO JOSE NEVES
MARIA LOUISA ACEVEDO PINTO
ALL CAME FROM (PORTUGAL) FROM THE
COLLEGIO INTERNATO DOS CARVALHOS, PORTO
DIANA COPPERWHITE (IRELAND) LIMERICK ART SCH.
SLAVILA SOBOTOVICOVA (SLOVAKIA) THE SLOVAKIAN
ACADEMY OF ARTS, BRATISLAVA
PABLO VILLANVEVO OTERO (SPAIN)
FROM FACULTATE DE BELA
ARTES, VIGO.
DAVID ROWLANDS, CARDIFF
SCHOOL OF ART, CARDIFF

ARTHUR WATSON, DIRECTOR OF
PEACOCK PRINTMAKERS
ABERDEEN — MARY MODEEN
DUNCAN OF JORDANSTONE
COLLEGE OF ART WERE
DIRECTORS OF THE
PRINTMAKING
MASTER CLASS

STRASBOURG CATHEDRAL

Richard Demarco '92

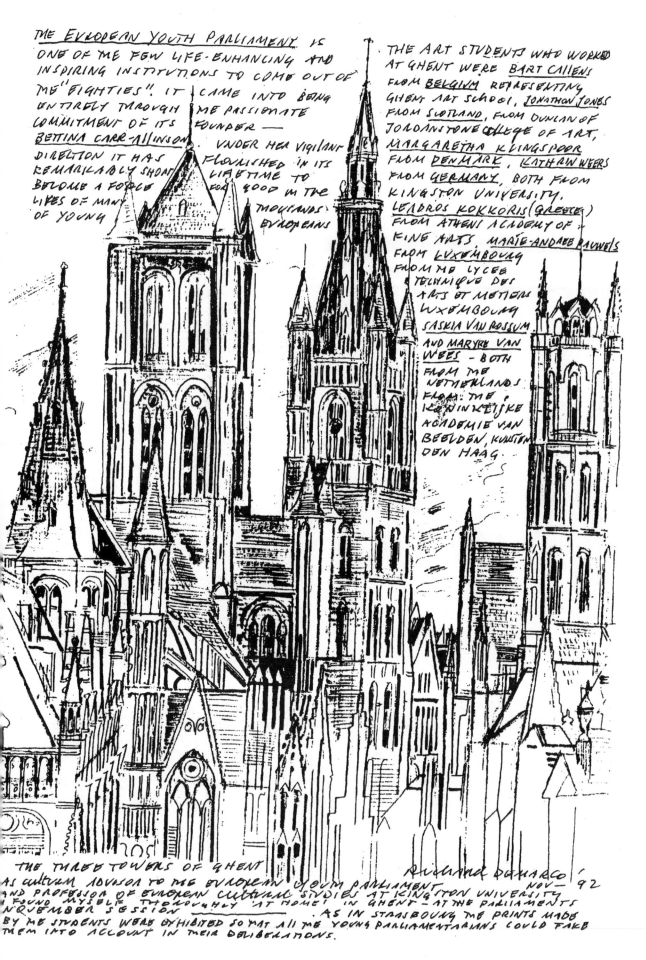

THE EUROPEAN YOUTH PARLIAMENT IS ONE OF THE FEW LIFE-ENHANCING AND INSPIRING INSTITUTIONS TO COME OUT OF THE "EIGHTIES". IT CAME INTO BEING ENTIRELY THROUGH THE PASSIONATE COMMITMENT OF ITS FOUNDER — BETTINA CARR-ALLINSON. DIRECTION IT HAS REMARKABLY SHORT BECOME A FORCE LIVES OF MANY OF YOUNG. UNDER HER VIGILANT FLOURISHED IN ITS LIFETIME TO FOR GOOD IN THE THOUSANDS EUROPEANS

THE ART STUDENTS WHO WORKED AT GHENT WERE BART CALLENS FROM BELGIUM REPRESENTING GHENT ART SCHOOL, JONATHAN JONES FROM SCOTLAND, FROM DUNCAN OF JORDANSTONE COLLEGE OF ART, MARGARETHA KLINGSPOOR FROM DENMARK, KATHRYN WEERS FROM GERMANY, BOTH FROM KINGSTON UNIVERSITY. LEANDROS KOKKORIS (GREECE) FROM ATHENS ACADEMY OF FINE ARTS. MARIE-ANDRÉE PAUWELS FROM LUXEMBOURG FROM THE LYCÉE TECHNIQUE DES ARTS ET MÉTIERS LUXEMBOURG SASKIA VAN ROSSUM AND MARYKE VAN WEES — BOTH FROM THE NETHERLANDS FROM THE KONINKLIJKE ACADEMIE VAN BEELDEN, KUNSTEN DEN HAAG.

THE THREE TOWERS OF GHENT

Richard Demarco
Nov — 92

AS CULTURAL ADVISOR TO THE EUROPEAN YOUTH PARLIAMENT AND PROFESSOR OF EUROPEAN CULTURAL STUDIES AT KINGSTON UNIVERSITY I FOUND MYSELF THOROUGHLY "AT HOME" IN GHENT - AT THE PARLIAMENTS NOVEMBER SESSION _____ . AS IN STRASBOURG THE PRINTS MADE BY THE STUDENTS WERE EXHIBITED SO THAT ALL THE YOUNG PARLIAMENTARIANS COULD TAKE THEM INTO ACCOUNT IN THEIR DELIBERATIONS.

169

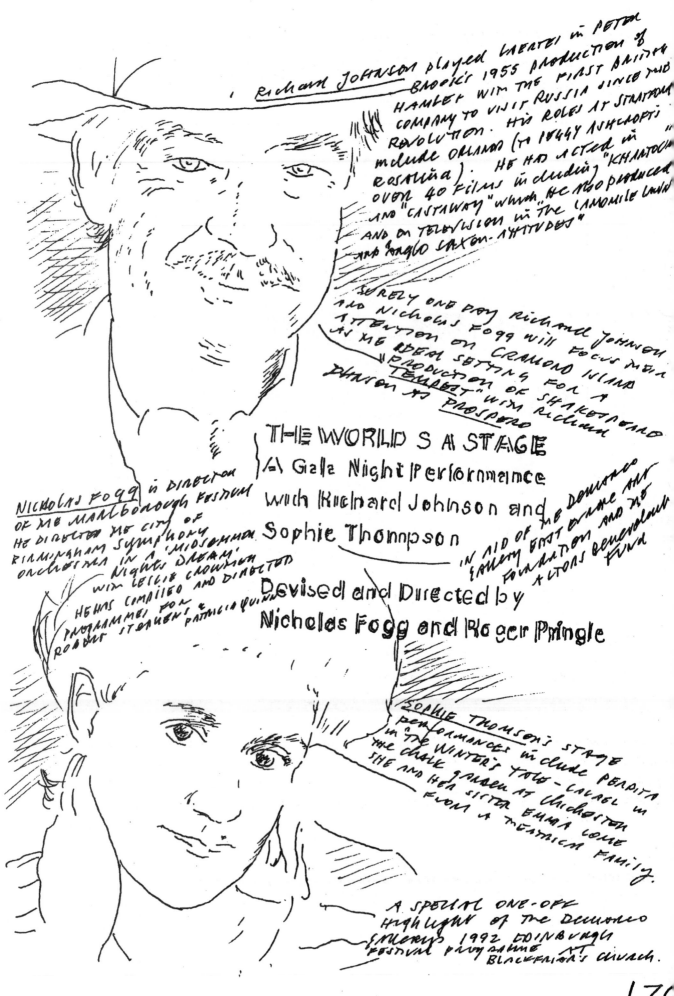

Richard JOHNSON played LAERTES in PETER BROOK'S 1955 PRODUCTION of HAMLET WITH THE FIRST BRITISH COMPANY TO VISIT RUSSIA SINCE THE REVOLUTION. HIS ROLES AT STRATFORD include ORLANDO (TO 1944 ASHCROFT'S ROSALIND). HE HAS ACTED IN OVER 40 FILMS including "KHARTOUM" AND "CASTAWAY" WHICH HE ALSO PRODUCED AND ON TELEVISION IN THE CAMOMILE LAWN AND ANGLO SAXON ATTITUDES"

SURELY ONE DAY Richard JOHNSON AND NICHOLAS FOGG WILL FOCUS THEIR ATTENTION ON CRAMOND ISLAND AN IDEAL SETTING FOR A "PRODUCTION OF SHAKESPEARE'S "TEMPEST" WITH Richard JOHNSON AS PROSPERO

THE WORLD'S A STAGE
A Gala Night Performance
with Richard Johnson and
Sophie Thompson

IN AID OF THE DEMARCO GALLERY EDIT DRAME ART FOUNDATION AND THE ACTORS BENEVOLENT FUND

NICHOLAS FOGG is DIRECTOR OF THE MARLBOROUGH FESTIVAL HE DIRECTED THE CITY OF BIRMINGHAM SYMPHONY ORCHESTRA IN A 'MIDSUMMER NIGHTS DREAM' WITH LESLIE CROWTHER HE HAS COMPILED PROGRAMMES FOR ROBERT STEPHENS AND PATRICIA QUINN

Devised and Directed by
Nicholas Fogg and Roger Pringle

SOPHIE THOMSON'S STAGE PERFORMANCES include PERDITA in THE WINTER'S TALE-LAUREL in THE CHALK GARDEN AT CHICHESTER SHE AND HER SISTER EMMA COME FROM A THEATRICAL FAMILY.

A SPECIAL ONE-OFF HIGHLIGHT OF THE DEMARCO GALLERY'S 1992 EDINBURGH FESTIVAL PROGRAMME AT BLACKFRIAR'S CHURCH.

CHAMBER ENSEMBLE FOR OLD BULGARIAN & SLAVONIC CHANTS

WITH FINANCIAL SUPPORT FROM THE BULGARIAN EMBASSY, PHILIPPOPOLIS AND THE DEMARCO EAST EUROPEAN ART FOUNDATION.

THE DEMARCO GALLERY RECITAL SERIES LAUNCHED AT ONE OF SCOTLAND'S PREMIER CONCERT & RECITAL VENUES — ST. MARY'S EPISCOPAL CATHEDRAL — EDINBURGH — FOR THE 1992 EDINBURGH FESTIVAL — THE UNIQUE & LEGENDARY PHILIPPOPOLIS CHOIR MARK A MUSICAL WATERSHED IN THE DEMARCO GALLERY'S CONTINUING DIALOGUE WITH THE COUNTRIES OF WHAT WAS THE OLD "EASTERN BLOC" — THE FOURTEEN CHOIR MEMBERS GAVE 3 CONCERTS AT THE FESTIVAL AND AS PART OF A TOUR OF THE BRITISH ISLES PERFORMED IN THE IDEAL SETTINGS OF ETON COLLEGE CHAPEL AND DOWNSIDE ABBEY. THE BULGARIAN AMBASSADOR IN BRITAIN H.E. IVAN STANCIOFF AND THE CULTURAL ATTACHÉ AT THE BULGARIAN EMBASSY, AGLIKA MARKOVA WORKED HARD TO MAKE THIS ONE OF THE MOST MEMORABLE EXPERIENCES OF THE 1992 EDINBURGH FESTIVAL

"THE TALKING TONGUES" THEATRE COMPANY CAME INTO
BEING AT CAMBRIDGE UNIVERSITY WHEN DAVID FARR
ROSE GARNETT, SASHA HAILS AND RACHEL WEISZ
BECAME FRIENDS AS UNDERGRADUATES. THEY WON
ACCLAIM AND THE GUARDIAN NEWSPAPER'S HARA AWARD
AT THE 1991 EDINBURGH FESTIVAL WITH THEIR PRODUCTION
OF 'SLIGHT POSSESSION'

SHAMELESS EXTRAS
IS ABOUT THE MEETING
OF TWO YOUNG
WOMEN INVOLVED
IN A BATTLE OF
TWO OPPOSING
PERSONALITIES

THEIR ATTITUDE
TOWARDS
EACH OTHER
IS OFTEN
COMICAL
BUT UNDERLYING
ALL THEIR
ACTIONS IS
THE PERVERSITY
WHICH
THREATENS
TRAGEDY

THEY RETURNED TO THE
Demarco Gallery's FESTIVAL
PROGRAMME IN 1992 WITH THEIR
PRODUCTION OF "TALKING TONGUES
NOT LONG AFTER THEY HAD PERFORMED
AT THE NATIONAL COTTESLOE THEATRE

172

"GET ON YOUR KNEES FOR A TICKET.... YVETTE BOZSIK IS THE GREAT DISCOVERY OF THIS YEAR'S EDINBURGH FESTIVAL" — SO WROTE JOHN LINKLATER THE GLASGOW HERALD THEATRE CRITIC IN 1993

I PLAN TO PRESENT YVETTE BOZSIK IN A MASTER CLASS PROGRAMME IN HER NATIVE CITY OF BUDAPEST IN THE ALMASSY PALACE WHICH HOUSES THE HUNGARIAN OFFICE OF THE KINGSTON DEMARCO EUROPEAN CULTURAL FOUNDATION

AS PART OF MY WORK AS PROFESSOR OF EUROPEAN CULTURAL STUDIES AT KINGSTON UNIVERSITY I WAS PLEASED TO SEE YVETTE BOZSIK CONDUCT A MASTER CLASS AND HOLD THE ATTENTION OF 200 STUDENTS. SHE SPOKE ABOUT "SOIRÉE" HER DANCE-THEATRE-SCULPTURE INSPIRED BY SARTRE'S "HUIS CLOS". THIS WAS AWARDED THE TITLE OF "BEST DANCE PRODUCTION" OF THE WHOLE EDINBURGH FESTIVAL 1993 — BOTH OFFICIAL AND FRINGE

WHEN I FIRST EXPERIENCED HER GENIUS, ON MY VISIT TO THE BUDAPEST SPRING FESTIVAL IN 1988 I RECOGNISED HER WORK TOOK INTO ACCOUNT THE CHALLENGE IMPLIED IN THE AVANT-GARDISM OF BOTH JOSEPH BEUYS AND TADEUSZ KANTOR. I SAW HER NOT AS "A DANCER, NOR EVEN AS AN ACTRESS BUT AS AN EXPONENT OF PERFORMANCE ART" MAKING <u>SCULPTURE</u>.

173

DEA FOUNDATION 1995 EDINBURGH FESTIVAL PROGRAMME
AT EDINBURGH COLLEGE OF ART

THE ATTORNEY PROJECT:
JOHN LATHAM, ARTIST
PHYSICS vs PHILOSOPHY THEOLOGY AND TRACQUAIR

JOHN LATHAM ASKING THE QUESTION
OF SCIENTISTS, THEOLOGIANS, PHILOSOPHERS,
"DOES SCIENCE SUBSUME ART OR DOES
ART SUBSUME SCIENCE?"

A ONE-DAY 'ACTION' IN THE FORM
OF A LEGAL DEBATE CONDUCTED BY
THE SCOTTISH ADVOCATE
JOHN X. SIMPSON IN THE
LECTURE ROOM
OF EDINBURGH
COLLEGE OF
ART

THE IMAGE OF
JOHN LATHAM'S "BOOK"
RELFECTED ON THE
WALL

CELEBRATING THE 250 ANNIVERSARY OF THE PERFORMANCE
OF THE SCOTTISH SYMPHONY — CELTIC KINLOCH RANNOCH
PRESENTED IN A LIVE-DRAWING ROOM AT EDINBURGH COLLEGE
OF ART IN AUGUST 1970

HENNING CHRISTIANSEN AND URSULA REUTER
PERFORM THEIR ACTION IN THE VERY SAME
LIFE ROOM WHERE JOSEPH BEUYS IN
COLLABORATION WITH
HENNING CHRISTIANSEN
FIRST PERFORMED THE
SCOTTISH SYMPHONY

URSULA REUTER

WITNESSES PARTICIPATING IN THE ATTORNEY PROJECT: DR. RUTH PAGE, NEW COLLEGE EDINBURGH
JOHN PEACOCK, PROF. OF ASTRONOMY, UNIV. OF EDINBURGH, MELHIBALD ROY, PROF. EMERITUS GLASGOW
DAVID SAXON, KELVIN PROF. OF PHYSICS, UNIV. OF GLASGOW

VASILI VASILIEV ARTIST FROM VITEBSK

VYTAUTIS LANDSBERGIS

ABDELAI DIOURI

JOHN LATHAM

JOHN LATHAM 'BOOK' SCULPTURE

GENERAL NOTES ON THE VISUAL
ARTS PROGRAMME OF THE DEA FOUNDATION
FOR THE 1995 EDINBURGH FESTIVAL

JOHN LATHAM DISCUSSING HIS
EXHIBITION AT EDINBURGH COLLEGE OF ART
WITH VYTAUTIS LANDSBERGIS, MODEHAI DOURI OF UK
AND THE CONTEMPORARY CULTURAL LIFE OF
LITHUANIA, MOROCCO AND BELARUS.
JOHN LATHAM IS EXPLAINING
HIS SCULPTURAL PROJECT
WHICH HE CALLS THE "NIDDRY WOMAN"
BEINGS OF WEST LOTHIAN INTO
A LARGE-SCALE ARTWORK
CELEBRATING THE PRETENCE
OF THE EARTH GODDESS
IN THE LANDSCAPE — A PROJECT
WHICH INVOLVED HIM IN CLOSE
COLLABORATION WITH THE SCOTTISH OFFICE
AND WITH HIS WIFE BARBARA STEVENI.

THREE ARTISTS REMIXTORING

ANOTHER IMAGE OF GATES OTHER THAN THE FAMOUS TRAQUAIR "BEAR GATES"
THOSE WHICH BONNIE PRINCE CHARLIE
REQUESTED SHOULD NEVER BE
OPENED AFTER THIS DEPARTURE
FROM TRAQUAIR IN 1745
UNTIL A JACOBITE MONARCH
REGAINED THE BRITISH THRONE

KEVIN DAGGS GATE SCULPTURE
ONE OF HIS CONTRIBUTIONS TO THE "URSA MAJOR"
SCULPTURE PROJECT CONCEIVED BY PATRICK HEALEY FOR
FLORA AND CAROLINE MAXWELL STUART'S GARDEN AT TRAQUAIR

174

THE WORK OF 23 LITHUANIAN CONTEMPORARY ARTISTS INTRODUCED
INTO BRITAIN WITH THE FINANCIAL SUPPORT OF VISITING ARTS

"DUONA IR DRUSKA" — MEANING "BREAD AND SALT"

— THE FIRST EVER EXHIBITION OF LITHUANIAN CONTEMPORARY ART
PRESENTED IN BRITAIN — PRESENTED BY THE DEA FOUNDATION AND THE
EDINBURGH COLLEGE OF ART FOR THE 1995 EDINBURGH FESTIVAL
IN THE SCULPTURE COURT OF THE COLLEGE OF ART

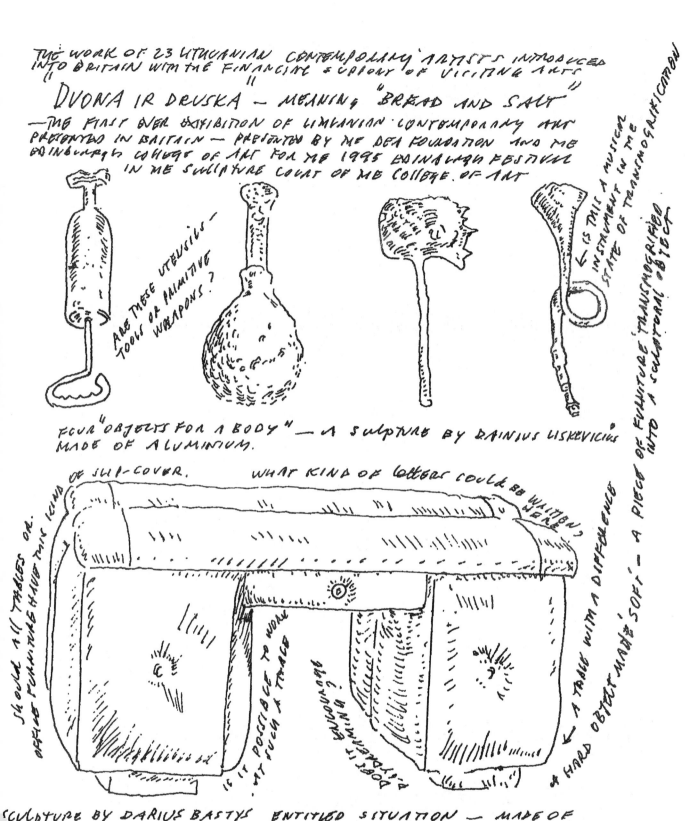

ARE THESE UTENSILS / TOOLS OR PRIMITIVE WEAPONS?

IS THIS A MUSICAL INSTRUMENT IN THE STATE OF TRANSMOGRIFICATION

← IS THIS A PIECE OF FURNITURE TRANSMOGRIFIED INTO A SCULPTURAL OBJECT

FOUR "OBJECTS FOR A BODY" — A SCULPTURE BY DAINIUS LISKEVICIUS
MADE OF ALUMINIUM.

... OF SLIP-COVER.   WHAT KIND OF LETTERS COULD BE WRITTEN HERE?

SHOULD ALL TABLES OR OFFICE FURNITURE HAVE THIS ICON OF ...

IS IT POSSIBLE TO WORK AT SUCH A TABLE

DOES IT ENCOURAGE DREAMING?

← A TABLE WITH A DIFFERENCE

A HARD OBJECT MADE SOFT — A PIECE OF

SCULPTURE BY DARIUS BASTYS   ENTITLED   SITUATION — MADE OF
                              LINEN & STRAW COVERING AN ACTUAL TABLE

RAMINTA JURENAITE CURATED THE EXHIBITION AS DIRECTOR OF VISUAL ARTS
INITIATIVES FOR THE SOROS FOUNDATION IN LITHUANIA. SHE DID SO IN COLLABORATION
WITH THE ICELANDIC ARTIST BRYNDIS SNAEBJORNSDOTTIR. (IT SHOULD BE NOTED THAT
ICELAND WAS THE FIRST COUNTRY TO RECOGNISE LITHUANIA'S INDEPENDENCE.

I FIRST SAW THIS EXHIBITION AT THE THE NATIONAL GALLERY OF MODERN
ART IN VILNIUS ON MY FIRST VISIT TO LITHUANIA IN 1994 — MADE POSSIBLE
BY GABRIELLA CARDAZZO'S PERSONAL COMMITMENT TO SUPPORTING LITHUANIAN
ARTISTS. MY RETURN VISIT IN JANUARY 1995 ENABLED ME TO INTRODUCE
BRYNDIS SNAEBJORNSDOTTIR TO RAMINTA JURENAITE AND HER COLLEAGUES

175

IKON IN TIMISOARA CATHEDRAL MUSEUM

Richard Demarco

20/3
19/91

ON THE STEPS OF THIS CATHEDRAL CITIZENS OF TIMISOARA (PROTESTING AGAINST CEAUCESCU'S TYRANNY) WERE SHOT BY THE SECURITY FORCES... AND SO THE OVERTHROW OF CEAUCESCU BEGAN — IN THAT PART OF ROMANIA WHERE THERE IS A SIGNIFICANT HUNGARIAN COMMUNITY, CLOSE TO THE BORDER WITH HUNGARY.

AT THE BEGINNING OF THE
EDINBURGH ARTS
EXPEDITION FROM
BUDA..... TO
TIMIS...RA

8.15 AM 19/3 R DEMARCO
to 8.25 AM 19/91

THE WINDMILL'S SAILS

BELOW THE,
CRUCIFIX IS A
STATUE OF MARY THE
GRIEVING AT THE
DEATH OF HER SON

A PIECE OF ROADSIDE
RELIGIOUS SCULPTURE
UNTHINKABLE ON
THE OUTSKIRTS
OF BRITAIN'S
LATE 20TH CENTURY!!!
CITIES

ON THE OUTSKIRTS OF BUDAPEST IN THE SMALL TOWN OF KECSKEMÉT
THERE IS AN INN. IDEAL FOR BREAKFAST. THE INN HAS A THATCHED
ROOF. AND BESIDE IT IS A CROSS WITH THE CRUCIFIED CHRIST

TERRY NEWMAN IS A VETERN OF "EDINBURGH ARTS" STYLE EXPEDITIONS TO POLAND, ITALY, GERMANY, HOLLAND, FRANCE. SHE IS AN ARTIST WIM BELYSIAN SENSIBILITIES

SUZI MESZOLY - WHEN I FIRST MET HER WORKED FOR ME MUSARNOK GALLERY IN BUDAPEST. LATER SHE DIRECTED THE SOROS FOUNDATION IN HUNGARY. SHE IS AT HEART AN ARTIST.

TERRY NEWMAN & SUZANNE
AT LUNCH SUNDAY 17 MARCH
AT THE NEWLY-OPENED
RESTAURANT
"KISBUDA GYONGYE"
AT 34 KENYERES UTCA.

A MOMENT IN ME EDINBURGH ARTS STYLE EXPEDITION TO BUDAPEST IN WHICH TEN ARTISTS WERE INTRODUCED TO ME CONTEMPORARY VISUAL ART WORLD OF BUDAPEST. THROUGH AN EXHIBITION AT ME NATIONAL ART ACADEMY. ALL ME WORKS EXHIBITED WERE MADE IN THE SCULPTURE STUDIOS OF ME ACADEMY. THIS EXPEDITION WAS PART OF MY PLAN TO STRENGTHEN ACADEMIC LINKS BETWEEN ME ACADEMY AND KINGSTON UNIVERSITY SCHOOL OF ART AND DESIGN.

17

A COLLAGE-PAINTING

REBECCA HORN
AND JANNIS KOUNELLIS
IN COLLABORATION

AT "FOFI'S ESTIATORIO"

GEORGE WYLLIE, MARILYN JEFFCOAT AND KERENY MUNRO
AT DINNER WITH AXEL WOLKENHAUER AND TILL JUNKEL
IN A RESTAURANT LONG FAVOURED BY BERLIN'S ARTISTS

Richard Demarco

179

THE DEA FOUNDATION'S
1993 EDINBURGH FESTIVAL PROGRAMME
WAS ENHANCED BY AN EXHIBITION
ENTITLED
"WITNESSES OF
EXISTENCE"
PART ONE →
THIS LITTLE
SCULPTURE WAS
THE CENTRE PIECE

THERE ARE →
TWO EYES
MADE OF
BROKEN MIRROR
GLASS. IF
YOU LOOK
INTO THEM,
BECAUSE AT
A DISTANCE
THEY ARE
JEWELL-LIKE
YOU REALISE
THEY REFLECT
YOUR OWN
EYES.

THIS CIGARETTE CASE, SOMEHOW
SURVIVED THE SHELLING AND RESULTANT
FIRE WHICH LEFT THE OBALA GALLERY
A BURNT-OUT
SHELL.
IT IS SIGNED
BY THREE
MEMBERS OF
THE OBALA
GALLERY. MIRSAD
PURIVATRA (MIRO)
THE GALLERY
DIRECTOR, PETAR
WALDEGG AND
NUSRET PAŠIĆ

THEY GAVE IT NEW
LIFE BY MAKING IT
INTO A WORK OF
ART. SHEENA McDONALD
SMUGGLED IT AND
16 TINY PRINTS
OUT OF SARAJEVO
TO BRING IT SAFELY
TO ST. MARY'S SCHOOL

← A RED (BLEEDING HEART)
CAUGHT IN A TRAP
WHICH COULD BE
THE STEEP SLOPES
OF THE HILLS WHICH
SURROUND SARAJEVO
AND ENABLE THE
BOSNIAN-SERB
GUNNERS AND
SNIPERS TO FIRE
AT WILL UPON THE
CITY CENTRE.

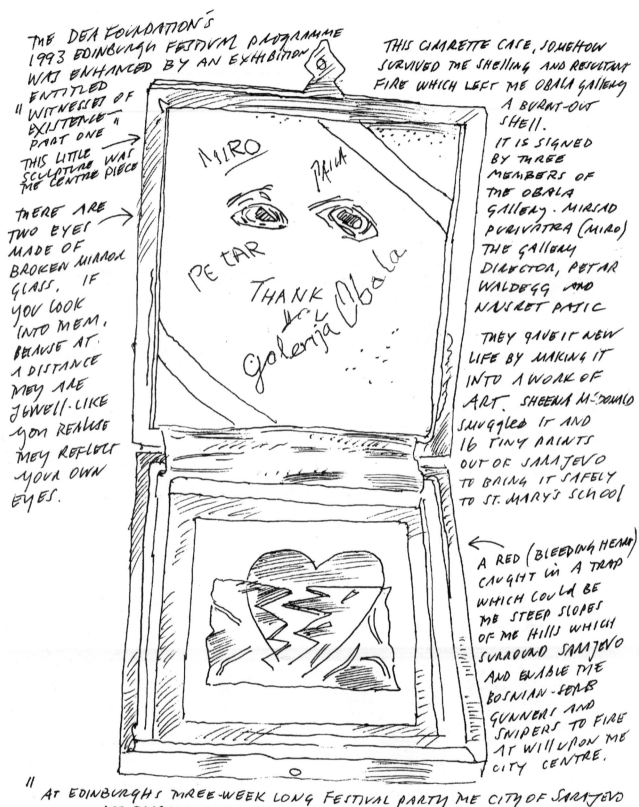

"AT EDINBURGH'S THREE-WEEK LONG FESTIVAL PARTY THE CITY OF SARAJEVO
IS THE GATE CRASHER WITHOUT A TIE STRUGGLING WITH THE BOUNCER AT
THE DOOR. BUT DESPITE THE NOISE FROM THE STEREO AND THE CLINK OF
GLASSES A FEW SHOUTED WORDS ARE GETTING THROUGH TO THE REVELLERS.
NOW AT THE RISK OF BEING PARTY-POOPERS SOME ARE ASKING HAS THE WORLD'S
BIGGEST ARTS FESTIVAL BETRAYED BOSNIA?"
SO WROTE SHEENA McDONALD ON HER RETURN FROM SARAJEVO
BEARING GIFTS FROM THE OBALA GALLERY ARTISTS TO THE DEMARCO FOUNDATION

180

MEMORIES OF ME BRIDGE OF MOSTAR   1988

INSPIRED BY ME EDINBURGH ARTS EXPEDITION TO SARAJEVO   Richard Demarco

AND MOSTAR VIA LJUBLJANA, ZAGREB & BELGRADE

181

THE ROCK OF GIBRALTAR
VIEWED FROM THE AIRPORT
running with clouds vapourising in a light BREEZE 14.12
17/94
under the light of a HALf moon.   — RICHARD DEMARCO

La Presse

TOILETTE

BAR/RESTAURANT LA PRESSE
CASABLANCA

Dec. 94   Richard DeMarco

WHEN ALAIN BOURDON TOOK ME HERE FOR LUNCH I discovered
THE SPIRIT OF HUMPHREY BOGART'S CASABLANCA.

A detail from the painting by the Moroccan painter - DRISSI

1995 EDINBURGH FESTIVAL EXHIBITION AT THE EDINBURGH COLLEGE OF ART
AN EXHIBITION OF MOROCCAN ARTISTS EXPRESSING IMAGES OF CASABLANCA

CASABLANCA. FRAGMENTS D'IMAGINAIRE

THE OTHER TWO EXHIBITIONS WERE PAINTING BY ABDELKRIM OUAZZANI AND PHOTOGRAPHS BY ALAIN GOURDON AND AZIZ SAYE A RETROSPECTIVE OF WORK BY THE BRITISH COUNCIL AND PHOTO DOVE

EXHIBITION CURATED BY ALAIN GOURDON AND AZIZ SAYE BY ANNE MARIE

THIS EXHIBITION WAS ONE OF THREE EXHIBITIONS DURING A MONTH
ESTABLISHED CULTURAL DIALOGUE BETWEEN MOROCCO AND SCOTLAND
ALL THREE RECEIVING FINANCIAL SUPPORT FROM VISITING ARTS -

AN EXHIBITION JOINTLY ORGANISED BY THE DEA FOUNDATION AND
THE BRITISH COUNCIL IN MOROCCO IN COLLABORATION WITH EDINBURGH
COLLEGE OF ART AND THE INSTITUT FRANÇAISE DE CASABLANCA
WITH THE SUPPORT OF CASABLANCA URBAN COMMUNITY. THE FONDATION
BANQUE POPULAIRE POUR L'EDUCATION ET LA CULTURE

184

OLD TOWN, RABAT MOROCCO   DEC. 94
                                    Richard DeMarco

185

THE BEAR GATES. TRAQUAIR.

18(

THE RESURRECTION

'THE RESURRECTION' IN TRAQUAIR CHAPEL.
16ᵀᴴ century Flemish OAK PANEL

187

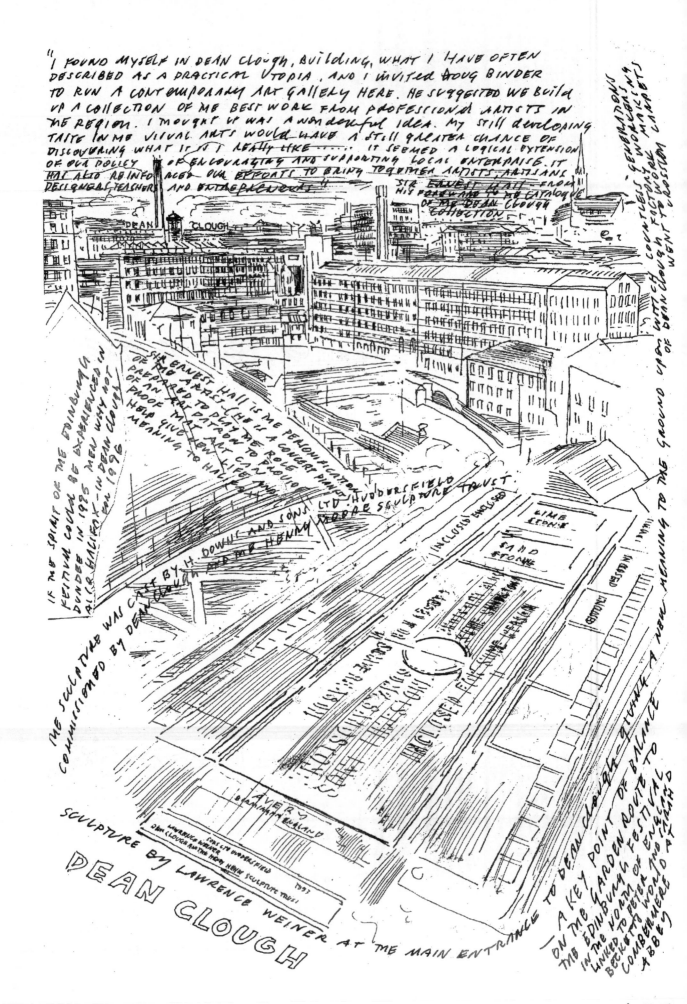

"I FOUND MYSELF IN DEAN CLOUGH, BUILDING, WHAT I HAVE OFTEN DESCRIBED AS A PRACTICAL UTOPIA, AND I INVITED DOUG BINDER TO RUN A CONTEMPORARY ART GALLERY HERE. HE SUGGESTED WE BUILD UP A COLLECTION OF THE BEST WORK FROM PROFESSIONAL ARTISTS IN THE REGION. I THOUGHT IT WAS A WONDERFUL IDEA. MY STILL DEVELOPING TASTE IN THE VISUAL ARTS WOULD HAVE A STILL GREATER CHANCE OF DISCOVERING WHAT IT IS I REALLY LIKE .... IT SEEMED A LOGICAL EXTENSION OF OUR POLICY OF ENCOURAGING AND SUPPORTING LOCAL ENTERPRISE. IT HAS ALSO REINFORCED OUR EFFORTS TO BRING TOGETHER ARTISTS, ARTISANS DESIGNERS, TEACHERS AND ENTREPRENEURS."

SIR ERNEST HALL FROM HIS FOREWARD TO THE CATALOGUE OF THE DEAN CLOUGH COLLECTION

COUNTLESS GENERATIONS OF COUNTLESS WORKERS WITH CITY FACTORY MAIDENS WENT TO DEAN CLOUGH TO EARN A CRUST

IF THE SPIRIT OF THE EDINBURGH FESTIVAL COULD BE EXPERIENCED IN DUNDEE IN 1995 WHY NOT ALSO HALIFAX IN DEAN CLOUGH FOR 1996

STR ERNEST HALL IS THE PERSONIFICATION OF THE ARTIST (HE IS A CONCERT PIANIST PREPARED TO PLAY THE ROLE OF AN ART PATRON TO PROVIDE PROOF THAT ART CAN HELP GIVE NEW LIFE AND MEANING TO HALIFAX)

THE SCULPTURE WAS CAST BY H. DOWNS AND SONS LTD, HUDDERSFIELD COMMISSIONED BY DEAN CLOUGH AND THE HENRY MOORE SCULPTURE TRUST.

INCLOSED ENCLOSED

LIME STONE

SAND STONE

AVERY BIRMINGHAM ENGLAND

LAWRENCE WEINER COLS LTD HUDDERSFIELD DEAN CLOUGH AND THE HENRY MOORE SCULPTURE TRUST 1997

A KEY POINT OF BALANCE TO DEAN CLOUGH — ITSELF A NEW MEANING TO THE GROUND UPON ON THE GARDEN ROUTE TO THE EDINBURGH FESTIVAL IN THE NORTH OF ENGLAND LINKED TO PETER WORLD AND BECKETH WORLD AND AT COMBERMERE WENT AT ABBEY

SCULPTURE BY LAWRENCE WEINER AT THE MAIN ENTRANCE

DEAN CLOUGH

THE PERFECT SETTING IN THE
BELOVED WORLD OF EDWARD THOMAS
FROM WHICH TO OBSERVE
THE CHRISTMAS ANGELS FLYING
AS THE YEAR 1995
COMES TO
AN END

A KEY POINT
IN THE SOUTH OF ENGLAND ON
IN COLLABORATION WITH MICHAEL AND
THE
TOLAI
GARDEN ROUTE TO THE EDINBURGH
BENSON COLDI
FESTIVAL

A GARDEN ELEGANTLY POSITIONED
BEAUTIFULLY CLOSE TO THE
WORLD OF DAVID AND JILL
YRULTON AT STEEP
AND DURFORD MILL
AND BEDALES SCHOOL

THE PERFECT SETTING
FOR THE UNIVERSITY
UNDER THE TREE
ENVIRONMENT
ENJOYED BY KINGSTON
UNIVERSITY PROFESSORS
RICHARD BENNATT
AND BRUCE RUSSELL

REFLECTION OF THE BETHLEHEM STAR OVER STONEHWOOD RICHARD DEMARCO '95

189

THE SPIRIT OF THE EDINBURGH FESTIVAL CAME
TO DUNDEE FOR THE FIRST TIME — AND NOT BEFORE
TIME — THANKS TO HAMISH GLEN AS DIRECTOR OF
DUNDEE REPERTORY THEATRE

THE SPIRIT OF REPERTORY THEATRE
descending upon
THE CITY OF DUNDEE
— FROM A SKETCH I PAINTED FOR THE NEWLY
OPENED DUNDEE REP THEATRE
IN 1963

DANIIL KHARMS
THERE TO BE HERE
A surrealistic play in two acts
Director - Oskaras Korsunovas
Composer - Gintaras Sodeika
Dramatization Oskaras Korsunovas
ACTORS:
Remigijus Bilinskas
Lina Budzeikaite
Algirdas Dainavicius
Audrius Hokas
Egila Sakalyte
Vygedas Telksnys
Rimante Valiuckaite
Audrius Zukas

THERE WAS ONLY ONE PLACE FOR THE
THEATRE OF OSKARAS KORSUNOVAS AND
THAT WAS DUNDEE REP
THEATRE

"... I am interested only in NONSENSE,
only in that which has no intelligible purpose;
I am interested only in the meaningless occurrences in life..."
— DANIIL KHARMS.

DANIIL KHARMS WAS MARTYRED
UNDER STALIN'S REGIME — A
RUSSIAN DISSIDENT WRITER
HE HAS LONG BEEN THE INSPIRATION
OF OSKARAS KORSUNOVAS — THE
YOUNG LITHUANIAN DIRECTOR
WHO OPERATES WITH
THE SPIRIT AND DEDICATION
OF A DEVOUT
FANATIC

THE PRODUCTION WAS TOO COMPLEX
AND TOO LARGE IN SCALE TO BE ENVISAGED
FOR ST. MARY'S SCHOOL.
IT WAS SO GOOD TO KNOW THAT
HAMISH GLEN WAS WELL ACQUAINTED
WITH LITHUANIAN AVANT-GARDE
THEATRE FROM HIS TIME
AS ARTISTIC DIRECTOR IN
VILNIUS AT THE VERY
HEIGHT OF RUSSIAN AVANT-
GARDE WHERE THE RUSSIAN
EXPERIENCE WAS
NON SCUM ... PRODUCTION

190

THE GATES SHOULD BE AN INVITATION
INTO A SACRED
AND SPIRITUAL
GARDEN.
WHERE MEMORIES
LINGER.

THE CHAPEL SHALL ECHO
THE SHAPE OF THE TREES
THEIR VERTICALITY —
A DANCE OF NATURE

A ROUGH SKETCH OF AN
IMAGINARY GATE —
INTO YOUR MEMORIAL
GARDEN.

4/94 R. DEMERID
19/95.

FOR MAGGIE WITH LOVE

191

" NEW BEGINNINGS
ARE IN THE
OFFING "

JOSEPH BEUYS.